Exploring Newspapers

David J. Walker

150th YEAR

MACMILLAN

First published 1993

Published by *Macmillan Publishers Limited*
London and Basingstoke

Typeset by Wearset, Boldon, Tyne and Wear

ISBN 0–333–57343–9

Printed in Hong Kong

A CIP catalogue record for this book is available from the British Library.

Contents

Contents

* denotes that the activity does not appear in the Student's Book, but as a suggestion in the Teaching Notes in the Self-Study edition.

To my parents, with love

Foreword

This book has its origins in the *Observer* EFL Service – later the Language Sector News Service – and many of the articles first appeared as part of the monthly packs of language materials distributed to subscribers. For this publication the worksheets have been considerably revised to include a wider range of activities. Notes and suggestions for exploiting the material have also been expanded and are included in the Self-Study edition.

Introduction

Who is the book for?

Exploring Newspapers is designed for students who have covered the groundwork of English grammar and syntax and who have a vocabulary which enables them to understand everyday conversations and read straightforward texts. It is, in other words, for students who have reached the 'intermediate' plateau and who now need to broaden their horizons.

What does it consist of?

The book consists of a selection of texts – both news reports and feature articles – taken from the British national press. These are accompanied by a variety of exercises and activities which exploit the material and provide opportunities for language practice. There are 40 units altogether, plus two quizzes – one at the half-way stage and one at the end.

What kind of topics?

The texts cover a wide range of topics, from fast food to keeping fit, from selling umbrellas in London to cycling holidays in France. In addition, there are a number of human-interest stories as well as articles which touch on issues of social concern. News reports of political events have not been included, however, since they tend quickly to lose their topical interest and become unrealistic for use as working texts.

What kind of language activities?

The accompanying language activities range from comprehension and vocabulary questions, through grammar and gap-fill exercises, to role-plays, discussions and suggestions for written work. The texts are interspersed with a series of matching exercises and jumbled cartoons – less demanding activities, which provide light relief.

How authentic are the texts?

The texts are completely authentic and have been reprinted from British newspapers unaltered for this book, apart from some updating of points of detail, such as prices. The articles and reports thus inevitably contain some challenging vocabulary at times, but they are mostly written in a direct and accessible style.

How are the units arranged?

The units may be done in any order but, for convenience, the slightly easier ones are placed at the beginning of the book and the more demanding ones at the end. The total ability range is not wide, however, and subject matter and exercise type may be a more practical and fruitful basis for selection. These can be readily referred to in the three indexes at the back.

What can students expect to gain from the book?

By exploring, with the help of the language activities, the range of newspaper texts presented in this book, students can expect to develop their English in a number of ways. They should achieve greater fluency in reading, broaden their vocabulary and understanding, and expand their means of expression, both in speaking and writing. They should also gain an insight into different styles of journalistic writing and, as a result, be able to approach with greater confidence the reading of newspapers and magazines in English.

Classroom use or private study?

The book is primarily intended for use in the classroom, many of the language activities being best performed in the context of discussion and the exchange of ideas. However, students working alone or with a private teacher will find much of practical linguistic value in the texts and the accompanying exercises, even if some of the activities, such as the role-plays and discussions, are precluded. The Self-Study edition contains general notes on the various exercise types as well as complete answers to all the questions and exercises. Practical teaching suggestions for exploiting each of the units are also given.

Note to the Student

As a general rule, try to read the text of each unit right through once, to get an overall idea of the content, before attempting to answer the detailed comprehension and vocabulary questions.

When answering the comprehension questions, try to avoid copying out sentences directly from the text. This does not really show how much you have understood, and will often miss the particular point of the question. Use the structure (especially the tense) of the question to frame your answer, but try to give the information in your own words. Remember that lengthy answers sometimes hide more than they reveal: short answers are often the best!

A number of the exercises refer to the use of a dictionary. You will find a good English–English dictionary not only useful for these particular activities, but also an invaluable companion as you read and work on the texts. As a general rule, however, try to deduce the meaning of a new word from its context before looking it up. Confirm (or, perhaps, correct) your impression by using the dictionary, and note other examples of the use of the word, as well as its definition. Check the pronunciation, too, and the position of the stress, if there is one.

I hope that, whether working with a group or studying privately, you will find this book useful in developing and expanding your English, and that you will enjoy using it. I hope, too, that you will realise that newspaper articles are not always quite as difficult as they may at first appear, and that you will be stimulated to explore for yourself the wide variety of newspapers and periodicals that are published in English.

General Notes for the Teacher

While it is hoped that the following general notes will be of some help and interest to all teachers using this book, they have been written with the less experienced teacher particularly in mind. They should, of course, be read in conjunction with the more detailed notes on each unit.

A 'Special' Units

1 Matching Headlines

There are three Matching Headlines units, all involving items of news-in-brief and two-word headlines. Even headlines as comparatively simple as these show some of the techniques of the sub-editor – the blocking of nouns and the use of the pun, for example – and help to prepare students for the more demanding types of headline encountered in all shades of the British press.

2 Matching Titles

These units require some careful reading of the texts as well as interpreting of the titles, but they are not difficult and can be used as light relief or 'fillers'. If time permits they could lead to discussions on television, radio and the cinema.

3 Cartoons

If possible, make photocopies of the cartoon, cut up the individual pictures and distribute to students in pairs. The students have half the pictures each and should then describe what they have to their partner, including reading out the text in the 'bubbles'. This is rather more difficult than simply laying the pictures down and moving them around, but it is more productive of language. Otherwise you find that students simply practise saying 'This one goes here' and 'That one goes there'! Don't forget to include the numbers, or else write them on the back.

4 Quizzes

It is not necessary to have covered all the units in class to do the quizzes. The unit numbers from which the questions are taken are given with the answers and so teachers can easily select questions relating to units that have been covered.

However, as the quizzes are not designed as memory tests – the information asked for is deliberately obscure – but rather as scanning exercises, the fact that a unit has not been covered need not preclude a question about it being asked: students can use the Contents List to try and identify the source – another scanning exercise en route! The most difficult questions to identify are those taken from the Headlines and Titles matching exercises, but teachers can guide appropriately or give page references in these cases.

B General Language Activities

There are notes and suggestions for most of the exercises and activities in the Teacher's Notes for each unit. If there are no notes for a particular exercise, it means that the exercise either is self-explanatory, or has clear instructions on the student pages.

1 Comprehension Questions

These are of various kinds, but they are not generally intended to be exercises in language manipulation, e.g. *The fire was caused by an electrical fault.* Question: *What caused the fire?* Their purpose is to help students towards a fuller and clearer understanding of the text – sometimes by asking about the general ideas or views being expressed, at other times by focusing attention on points of detail or the meaning that lies behind the words. If a text is straightforward, with little in the way of unusual syntax or indirectness of expression, there may be only a handful of questions, or sometimes none at all. In these cases the text is exploited in other ways – perhaps by using it as the basis for a role-play or as the starting point for a discussion.

Students should generally be encouraged and, if necessary, helped, to deduce meaning wherever possible. If you have doubts about using a text because you think the class may find it too difficult, try getting them to read the questions through first. This will often give students an overall feel of the content of the passage as well as provide them with key points to look for.

Students should always try to answer questions using their own words as far as possible. Copying out sentences wholesale from the text tends to make genuine comprehension difficult to assess, since it will often miss the particular focus of the question. Encourage students, however, to use the structure and tense of the question as a grammatical framework for their answer.

2 Vocabulary

In the vocabulary exercises, the selected words are those which the average intermediate student is unlikely to have come across but which have a certain frequency and are therefore of some practical value. This does not always mean that they should become part of their active vocabulary, but that students should at least add them to their stock of 'passive' words. Esoteric words which are not fundamental to the overall understanding of the text have not been included in the exercises. These can be ignored, guessed at or looked up by students at will.

3 Role-plays

There are eight set role-plays contained in the units. In the interview-type ones (Units 12, 17, 21, 25 and 28), begin by dividing the class into two groups, interviewers and interviewees, keeping them separate as far as possible at this stage.

The interviewers should prepare a list of questions, based on the information contained in the text. They can work in pairs or small groups and pool their ideas.

At the same time, the interviewees can study the text and prepare to be questioned. They should try to absorb the main facts and memorise them as far as possible. They, too, can work together, discussing any doubtful points, and test each other informally. Stress that they will not be able to look at the text during the role-play (this concentrates the mind wonderfully).

This preparation time (allow about 20–25 minutes) provides an invaluable opportunity for you to monitor students' progress and answer any queries. You should, of course, check that the interviewers' questions are accurately phrased and also that they are capable of being answered!

For the role-play itself, the students come together in pairs (they should not, ideally, know until this point who their opposite number is going to be). Encourage the interviewers to listen to the answers and to ask follow-up questions where appropriate – not just go through their list of questions! Interviewees should answer as freely and spontaneously as possible, and not refer to the text (brief notes of their own would be a compromise, but far better without). If students get stuck, they can always make up a (reasonable) answer. The interviewers should also be prepared to help out, by rephrasing the question, suggesting the answer, or moving on to another question.

In this kind of simultaneous role-play, monitoring everyone obviously becomes a problem but, if possible, record one or two of the interviews on a cassette and play back to the class for general feedback and follow-up. It adds greatly to the atmosphere of the recording and to students' performance if you record a brief sentence to set the scene, e.g. '. . . *and now we go over to our studio in London, where our reporter, 'X', is waiting to interview Mr 'Y'*. Alternatively, get one or two pairs to perform in front of the class; monitor, and give appropriate feedback.

A number of the suggestions outlined above also apply to the other three role-plays (Units 4, 6 and 35), but more specific notes can be found in the Teaching Notes to these units.

4   Discussions and Talking Points

During these speaking activities, encourage students to use any relevant new vocabulary and phrases encountered in the unit, perhaps by writing them on the board. In order to give more people a chance to contribute, a large class could divide into groups, each under its own chairperson; there could then be a general feedback session at the end. Further ideas for class discussions can be found in the 'warm-up' notes for each unit.

C   Pair- and Group-work

Many of the suggested exercises and activities lend themselves to students working together in class. Students can obviously gain much in this way, since they work in the language while in the process of exploring it and thus gain in confidence and fluency. Remember, however, that students need feedback, and that they do actually like to be taught from time to time! They need and like to improve their accuracy – in pronunciation and intonation as well as in structural usage and vocabulary – and they cannot expect (nor do they always particularly want) to get this from their peers. So, monitor groups as closely as possible and allow suitable time for feedback sessions.

D   Headlines and Predicting

Headlines in newspapers are designed to be eye-catching. This often involves an unusual or striking use of language, with the result that a headline may be more puzzling than informative – for native speakers as much as for the foreign learner. For this reason headlines are not always suitable for 'predicting' activities. They are often understood only <u>after</u> reading the article, when the play on words or special use of language becomes apparent and the sub-editor's wit can be appreciated.

The 'clever' headline is a feature of all shades of the British press and a number of examples are to be found in the units; attention is drawn to them in the Teaching Notes. Note that sometimes they form the basis of a comprehension question (<u>after</u> the passage has been read!).

Other headlines are more straightforward. Some, indeed, are quite long, reflecting the original layout of the article – maybe over a number of columns or across the top of a picture. These may well provide the opportunity for a prediction exercise, something which is left to the discretion of the teacher. However, as suggested above, care should be taken to avoid implying that the content of newspaper articles can always be deduced by studying the headlines.

E   Warm-ups

As headlines themselves do not always provide a suitable lead-in to an article, ideas for introducing the lesson from 'cold' can be found in the warm-up paragraphs at the beginning of the Teaching Notes to each unit. These are simply suggestions, and teachers may well find they can integrate some of the units into current class topics or themes. The warm-up period should be kept quite brief – it's only supposed to be an appetizer!

Note

In the Teaching Notes which accompany each unit in this Self-Study edition, I have tried to take into consideration the needs of the non-native teacher and the student working alone as well as the native teacher. For this reason, I have included explanations of some cultural and other references contained in the texts, including headlines, which might otherwise be obscure. By the same token, the suggestions in the warm-up notes and some of the discussions are given as much for the language they contain as for the ideas themselves, which claim no special originality.

Acknowledgements

The author and publishers wish to thank the following who have kindly given permission for the use of copyright material:

BBC Enterprises Ltd. for an adapted extract from 'No. 10 Downing Street' by Christopher Jones; BBC Magazines for two articles from the *Radio Times*, 'Wheels of Fortune' by Judi Goodwin (3 May 1986) and 'Pat takes good care of them' by Nicki Household (8 November 1986), and programme details in the *Radio Times* of TV and radio broadcasts; *In Britain* magazine for the article 'Shaping up nicely'; Independent Newspaper Publishing plc. for the report 'Red Arrows jet crashes into row of houses' by Mark Rosselli from *The Independent* (17 October 1987) and the article 'Teaching scientists to see with the eyes of a journalist' by Andrew Crane from *The Independent* (17 August 1987); Knight Features on behalf of United Features Syndicate Inc. for the 'Peanuts' cartoons; Ewan MacNaughton Associates on behalf of *The Telegraph* plc. for the articles 'Heavenly Piece of Kentucky Fried Chicken' by Tim Luard (13 November 1987); 'Some people love it – some people don't' by Christine Doyle (3 February 1987); 'Brain trains give commuters chance to learn Japanese' by John Petty (16 October 1987); 'Jailed umbrella man refused to fold up his brollies and go' by David Millward (21 November 1986); 'Drugs gang held after £51 million cocaine seizure' by Neil Darbyshire (27 November 1987); '110-year-old tourist' (27 August 1987), and 'Telling a good joke is serious business' by Jenny Rees (25 August 1987); The Observer Ltd. for the article 'Why the stars of rock who sing of their pain might actually mean it' by Annabel Ferriman from *The Observer* (7 June 1992); Rex Features Ltd. on behalf of *Today* Newspaper for the articles 'On foot to the roof of the world' by Andrew Morgan from *Sunday Today* (4 January 1987) and 'Triumph of kidnap Jenny' by Stewart Payne and Jenny Rees from *Today* (17 April 1986); Solo Syndication & Literary Agency Ltd. for the report 'Battle against the disaster in the night' featured in the *Daily Mail* (17 October 1987); The Spectator (1828) Ltd. for the article 'Deep in domesticity' by Jeffrey Bernard from *The Spectator* (April 1986); Desmond Wilcox Productions Ltd. for the photograph of Pat Kerr by Desmond Wilcox.

The author and publishers acknowledge with thanks the following photographic sources for the use of copyright material:

Allsport (Gary M. Prior) p.43; Associated Press/Topham Picture Source p.54; Barbara Daly p.6 (centre); Barnaby's Picture Library p.85 (bottom); Desmond Wilcox Productions Ltd. p.57; Empics p.80; Ewan MacNaughton Associates for *Daily Telegraph* pp.9, 11; Robert Harding Picture Library pp.2, 30, 85 (top); Hulton-Deutsch Collection pp.6 (left), 89; Hutchison Library (C. Woodhead) p.39; James Davis Travel Photography p.65; *The Observer* (John Hodder) p.16, (Murdo Macleod) p.34, (John Wildgoose) pp.24, 35; Picturepoint p.50; Popperfoto pp.22, 47; Quadrant Picture Library p.67; Topham Picture Source pp.6 (right), 24, 90.

Every effort has been made to trace all the copyright holders, but if any have been inadvertently overlooked the publishers will be pleased to make the necessary arrangements at the first opportunity.

Matching Headlines

Each of the nine news stories printed below should have a two-word headline – a word from Group A followed by a word from Group B. Study the news stories and then write the appropriate headline above each one, as in the example.

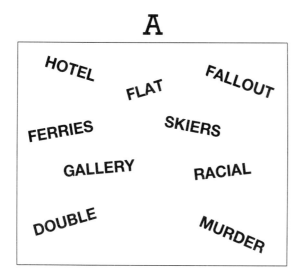

A

HOTEL   FLAT   FALLOUT
FERRIES   SKIERS
GALLERY   RACIAL
DOUBLE   MURDER

B

ACCORD   HIT
RAID
KILLING   BLAST
LINGERS   TROUBLE
PROBE   HURT

RACIAL ACCORD

Black and white leaders in South Africa agreed a blueprint for power-sharing talks.

1

Sheffield police are hunting the killer of Tina Marie Fletcher, 19, whose body was found at a flat near the city centre.

2

Three Post-Impressionist paintings worth £70,000 by Adrion, Foubert and Marchand were stolen from an art gallery in the West End of London.

3

Two cable cars at the French Alps ski resort of Les Orres fell 40ft, injuring 31 people, after the top of a pylon broke.

4

Brittany Ferries cancelled services for St Malo and Caen after strikes threats by French seamen.

5

Radiation at more than twice the recommended safety limit still affects 288,000 sheep on 407 Welsh farms, more than five years after the Chernobyl disaster.

6

A John Major lookalike, who tricked a nine-year-old Malvern girl of £32, was being sought by police.

7

At least three people were killed and 20 injured when an explosion believed to have been caused by gas tore through a hotel at Garmisch-Partenkirchen, a ski resort in the Bavarian Alps.

8

Detectives investigating the death of British seaman David Moon, 37, aboard ship off Brunei, fly to the Gulf today.

9

Matching Headlines

See General Note on page xii. These two-word headlines are fairly simple and demonstrate the flexibility of English – for example, the way in which nouns can be used as adjectives.

Note on the text
Paragraph 7 – John Major is the British Prime Minister.

A Heavenly Piece of Kentucky Fried Chicken

TRADITIONAL lion dances and crashing cymbals greeted the formal opening in Peking yesterday of the world's largest Kentucky Fried Chicken shop.

"The one, the only, the original recipe" proclaimed the hoardings, as sinuous dancers
10 waved red scarves and hundreds of balloons were released over Tiananmen Square in the heart of the Chinese capital.

"The Chinese have some of the finest dishes in the world – now they have one more," said Mr Richard Mayer, chairman of the American fast food
20 chain.

From the top of the new three-storey restaurant, the jolly, bespectacled features of the company's founding father, Col. Sanders, look out across the vast square towards the portrait of Chairman Mao, on The Gate of Heavenly Peace.

30 The present Communist party authorities say the welcome given to Kentucky Fried Chicken is in line with the policy of opening to the outside world, reaffirmed at the party congress earlier this month.

The restaurant, a joint venture with two Chinese state
40 corporations, seats 500 and can serve 2,000 chicken pieces an hour. The menu is the same as in 57 other countries.

Four policemen seen tucking into the cartons of chicken, mashed potato and coleslaw said with some surprise: "It tastes not bad."

Other customers, however,
50 found the secret blend of 11 herbs and spices somewhat less than finger-lickin' good. "I felt sick at the smell of it," said one.

In a city where a bowl of hot noodles or dumplings costs a few pence, a meal at the American fast-food store costs up to £2, a week's wages for
60 many Chinese.

A Heavenly Piece of Kentucky Fried Chicken

A   Comprehension

Read the article right through and then choose the best answer for each of the following. They are quite easy, so see first of all if you can do them from memory.

1   The ceremony which officially opened the first Kentucky Fried Chicken shop in China was
  a   dignified and formal.
  b   jolly and traditional.
  c   noisy and colourful.

2   The new restaurant is situated in
  a   Shanghai.
  b   Peking.
  c   we are not told where.

3   The Chinese authorities are welcoming Kentucky Fried Chicken because they
  a   want to be friends with America.
  b   like the idea of fast food.
  c   have decided to be more open to the world.

4   The policemen
  a   liked the food.
  b   didn't like the food.
  c   thought the food smelt awful.

5   A meal at the Kentucky Fried Chicken restaurant costs
  a   more than £2.
  b   as much as £2.
  c   about £2.

B   Vocabulary

1   Can you find a word or phrase in the text for each of the following?
  a   large boards for advertisements
  b   wearing glasses
  c   enormous
  d   a business enterprise with two or more partners
  e   eating enthusiastically
  f   it tastes so good you want to lick your fingers

2   Can you find the name of
  a   an item of clothing?
  b   a musical instrument?
  c   an animal?

3   In the headline, can you explain the use of the words *Heavenly Piece*?

C Grammar

Can you put *it tastes not bad* (lines 47–8) into correct English?

D Discussion

Do you like fast food? Which are your favourite fast-food restaurants? What are the characteristics of fast-food restaurants (apart from the obvious one of speed)? Compare these with the features of the more traditional restaurant.

A Heavenly Piece of Kentucky Fried Chicken

This short article about the opening of the first Western fast-food restaurant in China is quite straightforward, and should be within the capacity of lower-intermediate students.

Warm-up

Ask students what names of fast-food restaurants they know. In how many countries can you now eat Kentucky Fried Chicken? (58!). What is the name of the founder of this fast-food chain? (Colonel /kɜːnəl/ Sanders.) Can students describe him? (White-haired, bespectacled (see vocabulary exercise), smiling face . . .)

Headline

Note that this is the subject of question 3 in section B.

D   Discussion

What are the characteristics of fast-food restaurants? (Bright decor; self-service; young, cheerful (supposed to be!) staff; cheap prices; informality; use of cartons and paper plates (and fingers!); standard menus and prices – you know what to expect from a fast-food restaurant belonging to a particular chain.)

Compare the advantages and disadvantages of fast-food restaurants over the more traditional kind. Students may naturally divide into two camps, in which case a discussion should ensue! If not, ask them to think up arguments for the opposing point of view, perhaps working in groups to begin with, and then discussing/arguing with the other side.

ZOMBIE ON THE ROAD

Don't succumb to 'highway hypnosis' says **SUE BAKER**.

NEXT WEEKEND brings one of the year's big peaks for traffic on the roads, and with it the risk of the mesmerising effect of covering long distances on motorways.

The phenomenon is not new: it was first recognised in the 1960s in the United States, where the term 'highway hypnosis' was coined to describe it.

But the expansion of Britain's motorway network with the completion of the M25 may be encouraging many drivers to attempt greater mileages at a stretch this summer, to the concern of the Guild of Experienced Motorists. Driving on and on at a steady speed, a driver's level of alertness can deteriorate.

'Highway hypnosis' can cause the driver to start feeling detached, more like a spectator rather than the person actually controlling the vehicle.

As concentration ebbs, he or she starts to pay less attention to what is happening and everything seems to float by. A trance-like automation sets in. The serious danger then is that a combination of fatigue, the steady drone of the car and the somnolence of a warm day may actually make a driver nod off at the wheel.

The problem is so well recognised in Canada as a summer hazard that the Ontario Ministry of Transportations and Communications has issued a set of advisory rules to guide drivers.

Don't eat	comfortable clothing.
Talk to passengers	during normal sleeping hours.
Keep your eyes moving	in the car cool.
Take an interest	but not to the point of distraction.
Don't try to drive	and check your rear-view mirror often.
Keep the temperature	walking break every hour or so.
Avoid driving	in all road signs and traffic around you.
Take a coffee or	a heavy meal before driving.
Wear	too far in one day.

Matching Exercise

The 'advisory rules' mentioned in the last paragraph have become mixed up. Can you find the matching half for each of the nine rules?

Zombie on the road

The matching exercise is quite easy and can be done even by elementary students, independently of the newspaper extract. The latter contains a few difficult vocabulary items but the piece as a whole is not too demanding. It is very short and provides a good lead-in to the discussion.

Warm-up

Ask students if they enjoy driving on a motorway or a major highway. Do they prefer it to driving on ordinary roads? What are the advantages of the motorway or major highway? Are there any disadvantages?

Matching Exercise

This can be done either as a class activity or with students working together in pairs. After discussion, students could write out the nine sentences.

Vocabulary

1   Ask students to pick out from the text as many words as they can find which are associated with sleep, dreaming or tiredness. Encourage the use of dictionaries (English–English preferably) for this.
2   See if anyone can understand the significance of the car number plate in the illustration (quite difficult!)

Discussion

If not already explored in the warm-up, discuss other potential dangers of motorway driving.

Some people love it – some people don't!

A   Jeffrey Archer, novelist

B   Barbara Daly, make-up artist

C   Alice Thomas Ellis, novelist

"I TOOK UP exercise partly because my husband is dead keen, which made me feel I ought to do something, and partly because my doctor said aerobic exercise would alleviate the asthma I've suffered all my life. I now do three or four hours of aerobics each week, and I swim at the RAC club two or three evenings a week, too.

"I certainly feel better. I thought I was fit before, but this is quite a different experience.

"Exercise is also a great stress reliever. I can go to a class at 8.30pm feeling exhausted, and come out feeling marvellous. It's very important that the gyms I use are open late – and luckily I don't have to go too far out of my way to reach them.

"I think the answer is to do a moderate amount over a long period of time. Over-exercising isn't sensible, and it certainly isn't compatible with the life of a busy woman."

1

"I HATE exercise. I have done since school. Very few of my women friends take any exercise. My husband is a triple Blue, but it's different for men. It's natural for them to rush around.

"The closest I ever come to taking any exercise is walking down to the local shops to buy some more fags: I smoke about 40 a day. I don't worry about putting on weight, because I eat very little.

"I'm terribly healthy and I'm fitter than almost anybody I know. Reptiles live for ever because they do everything so slowly, and I'm sure that's what I'm like. Anyway, everybody brought up during the war is healthy. We didn't have any of the rubbish that people eat today."

2

"I USED to take athletics very seriously. I ran for Britain in the Sixties, and I still take a lot of exercise, not because I'm scared of having a heart attack or running to fat, but because I enjoy it. People tend to concentrate on things they are good at or enjoy, and I've been keen on sport since my father introduced me to cricket as a child.

"I play squash four times a week, including one session with my coach. I find jogging very boring, and pounding along pavements gives me sore shins, so on Saturdays I referee rugby matches, which gives me an hour and a half's running. In the summer I play cricket with the local third XI.

"I find all exercise very relaxing, and being physically fit helps in almost every area of your life. You eat better, sleep better, work better. I would have thought most people have worked that out by now."

3

STUART BIDDLE COMMENTS: a very defensive reaction. She is clearly generalising her unpleasant negative experience of sport and exercise at school to cover all forms of physical activity as an adult. Having failed in the past she doesn't want to risk failure again. Taking up exercise would also force her to consider the damage being built up by heavy smoking.

a

STUART BIDDLE COMMENTS: he is still competitive, hence the coach. He probably has a high level of physical self-confidence and wishes to maintain this image of himself when older. He probably finds jogging boring because, being extrovert, he prefers a more social, team approach.

b

STUART BIDDLE COMMENTS: a balanced approach and a perfect summary of much that I would agree with. She is motivated both on health grounds and socially, finding exercise both enjoyable and relaxing, even when feeling tired. What could be better?

c

Some people love it – some people don't!

Notes on the text

1   The *RAC* (passage 1) is the Royal Automobile Club (a British motoring organisation).

2   A *Blue* (passage 2) is a sporting honour, gained by representing either Oxford or Cambridge against the rival university. A 'triple Blue' is therefore someone who has represented his or her university in three different sports – a rare distinction. Oxford's colours are dark blue, Cambridge's light blue.

A   Matching Exercise

First, read texts 1, 2 and 3, in which three people describe their attitudes to exercise and physical fitness. Then look at the pictures and decide who wrote each one. Finally, study Stuart Biddle's comments and match them with the texts.

PICTURE	A	B	C
TEXT			
COMMENTS			

B   Grammar Revision

Note the use of the present tense, in all three texts, to describe everyday actions. (See Teaching Notes in the Self-Study edition for suggestions for practice.)

C   Pronunciation

In the text (paragraphs and comments) can you find

1   three words containing the sound /eə/ (as in *air*)?
2   four words containing the sound /ɪə/ (as in *ear*)?
3   five words containing the sound /e/ (as in *bed*) but spelt with the letters *ea*?

D   Pair Work

Working in pairs, ask each other questions about the attitudes to fitness of the three personalities featured.

E   Role-play

This time, still working in pairs, play the part of one of the personalities yourself and ask each other questions.

F   Dialogue

Working in pairs, and making use of the question structures and vocabulary you have practised in this unit, find out about each other's attitude to exercise, sport and physical fitness.

G   Writing Activity

Write a short piece about your own attitude to exercise, sport and physical fitness. (Don't write your name on it!) Make use, where you can, of some of the vocabulary and expressions in the texts, and remember that to talk about regular activities you will need the present simple tense.

Some people love it – some people don't!

This matching exercise is straightforward and is suitable for lower-intermediate students. It could be used as a follow-up to a lesson on the simple present, or for revision: the extracts contain a number of examples of 'everyday actions'. The suggested activities, both oral and written (see below), can be used to give students further practice.

Warm-up

Ask students about their attitudes to personal fitness. Do they think it important? How do they try and keep fit? Exercise? Sport? Jogging? What can make you unfit? Lack of exercise? Over-eating? Smoking? Drinking alcohol?

Vocabulary for checking/pre-teaching

to put on (and lose) weight
to take up (a sport, activity)
to be keen on something (**Note:** *dead keen* (paragraph 1) = very enthusiastic!)
a (sports) coach
stress
relief, to relieve

Students should be able to deduce the meaning of the word *fag*! (paragraph 2)

B   Grammar Revision

After checking the answers to the matching exercise, you could use the extracts to revise the third person singular of the present simple.

Examples:

1   How many hours of aerobics does Barbara Daly do each week? (She does three or four hours.)
2   How often does she swim at the RAC club? (Two or three evenings a week.)
3   How does she sometimes feel when she goes to an exercise class at 8.30? (She sometimes feels exhausted.)
4   How does she feel when she comes out? (Marvellous.)
5   Does Alice Thomas Ellis like exercise? (No, she hates it.)
6   What exercise does she do? (She walks down to the local shops.)
7   How many cigarettes does she smoke a day? (She smokes 40 a day.)
8   Does she worry about putting on weight? (No, she doesn't.)
9   Why not? (Because she eats very little.)
10   Why does Jeffrey Archer still take a lot of exercise? (Because he enjoys it.)
11   How often does he play squash? (He plays squash four times a week.)
12   Why doesn't he like jogging? (Because he finds it boring and it gives him sore shins.)

13 What does he do on Saturdays? (He referees rugby matches.)
14 What does he do in the summer? (He plays cricket.)

D Pair Work

After a question-and-answer session such as outlined above, students could work in pairs to gain practice at asking questions themselves. Make sure they know the difference between *How many . . . ?* and *How often . . . ?*

Student A asks student B about, say, Jeffrey Archer. Student B then asks student A about Barbara Daly, etc.
OR work in groups of three: student A asks student B about Jeffrey Archer, then student B asks student C about Barbara Daly, and student C asks student A about Alice Thomas Ellis.

E Role-play

In addition, or as an alternative to the above, students could take it in turns to 'play' one of the personalities and ask each other questions.

Examples: *How many cigarettes do you smoke a day?*
What do you do on Saturdays?

The best way to do this is to allow some preparation time. Students, in pairs, decide which personality each would like to be, and then prepare written questions to ask their partner, based on the relevant text. This gives the teacher a chance to circulate and check the question structures. Questions need not, of course, be limited to the present tense!

Students should also, of course, familiarise themselves with the text about the personality they are going to play. Ideally, the person interviewed should speak from memory (see General Note on page xiii), as this makes for a much more fluent and natural dialogue.

G Writing Activity

This exercise is suitable for more advanced as well as lower-level students.

As an extension to the exercise, collect the (anonymous!) written pieces and distribute them at random round the class. Each student then studies the text he/she is given and writes his/her own (expert!) comments at the bottom.

Finally, the work can be handed back to the original writers, who can then say what they think of the comments made – and find out who wrote them! If time permits, some could be read out to the class.

110-year-old tourist

BRITAIN'S oldest man made his first visit to London yesterday at the age of 110.

Mr John Evans, pictured below, had never found the time – or the money – to make the trip from his home in Fforestfach, near Swansea. But, when British Rail offered him an all-expenses-paid birthday treat to the capital he just could not refuse.

He arrived in style at Paddington station, smartly turned out in his best suit, favourite panama hat and a red rose in his buttonhole.

Sailed to Ilfracombe

"It's very exciting, there's no doubt about it," he said.

Until yesterday he had never been far from home, except for one trip to Aberdeen.

"But I've been on the seas to that faraway land called Ilfracombe 21 miles from home," he joked.

Mr Evans, who spent 60 years working as a miner in South Wales, almost made the journey to London once before, at the turn of the century.

"There was a trip to the White City but it was ten shillings return from Swansea – too much I thought. All my money went to the family then," he said.

During the next two days Mr Evans will be taken on a whistle-stop tour of London to see the sights. Top of his list is a visit to the Houses of Parliament organised by his MP, Mr Gareth Wardell.

The only arrangement he does not care for is the wheelchair provided to ferry him about if he gets tired. "I don't like the chair business – people will think I am getting old," he said.

His ingredients for a long and healthy life have been well publicised – no alcohol, no tobacco and no cursing.

Before setting off from Swansea with his 76-year-old son, Amwel, he quipped: "I'm glad to see they've given me a return ticket."

110-year-old tourist

A Memory Test

After reading the article about John Evans, Britain's oldest man, test your memory on the following exercise.

1 How old is Mr Evans?
2 Which is the nearest city to where he was born?
3 Which London station did he arrive at?
4 What did he wear in his buttonhole?
5 Mr Evans worked for sixty years. What was his job?
6 Why didn't he go to London before, when he had the chance?
7 Which special place is he going to see in London?
8 Why doesn't he like going about in a wheelchair?
9 Name two of Mr Evans's secrets for a long and healthy life.
10 How old is Mr Evans's son?

B Vocabulary

What is the meaning of the following words and phrases as they are used in the text?

1 *a treat* (line 11)
2 *smartly turned out* (lines 14–15)
3 *a whistle-stop tour* (lines 39–40)
4 *MP* (line 43)
5 *ingredients* (line 51)
6 *to curse* (line 54)
7 *to set off* (line 55)
8 *to quip* (line 57)

C Project

Apart from London, three places are mentioned in the article: Swansea, Aberdeen and Ilfracombe.

1 Look them up in an atlas to see exactly where they are. Which countries are they in? And what do they have in common?

2 Find out what you can about each place – from an encyclopaedia, or perhaps from a travel agent's brochure or from a tourist office.

3 EITHER
   a write a short paragraph about each place
   OR
   b give a brief talk about the place you would most like to visit.

D General Knowledge

Paddington is one of British Rail's London terminal stations. How many others can you name? You will do well if you can think of six without looking them up, but there are fifteen altogether!

110-year-old tourist

This short piece about Britain's oldest man should present little difficulty – it could probably be attempted by elementary students by turning the memory test into a normal comprehension exercise. The vocabulary and syntax are mostly very straightforward, with a number of examples of direct speech. The few words and expressions which might be unfamiliar are highlighted in the vocabulary exercise.

Note on the text
The White City (line 33) is the name of a sports stadium in West London.

Warm-up

Ask students if they know the age of the oldest man or woman in their country, or in the world. (113 would appear to be the highest verified claim.) In which part of the world are people reputed to live to a great age? (Georgia.) In what ways would life have been different at the end of the last century, compared with now?

Jailed umbrella man refused to fold up his brollies and go

By David Millward

AFTER spending nearly four weeks in Pentonville Prison for breaking his High Court undertaking not to carry on street trading in the City of Westminster, Ronald Jordan was back at work yesterday.

Although his chosen pitch, Leather Lane, near Holborn 10 Circus, was in the neighbouring borough of Camden, Jordan made it clear he would soon be back in the West End, whether Westminster City Council liked it or not.

His return to work was delayed by a little unfinished business – an appearance before Thames Magistrates – 20 where he was fined £50 after admitting two charges of obstructing Whitechapel High Street on Oct. 19.

Jordan, 44, of Squires Lane, Finchley, veteran of countless court appearances, was greeted with a measure of resignation by the magistrate, Mr Terence Maher. "Are 30 you up to date with your fines?" he asked. "No doubt we will see you again."

Having asked for seven days to pay, Jordan – a street trader for 23 years – went about his business. With London bathed in sunshine, umbrellas – a snip at £3 and £3.50 – were left in the van, 40 illegally parked on a yellow line.

Yet within minutes office workers were crowding round his pitch. Trade in musical bunnies, dolls, rubber snakes and assorted other novelties was brisk.

Jordan became the first street trader to be imprisoned 50 under Westminster council's new policy of seeking High Court injunctions when he appeared in the High Court for the third time on Oct. 23.

Street trader Ronald Jordan operating legally in Leather Lane, Holborn, yesterday, after his four-week spell in Pentonville prison.

His enthusiasm, however, remains undimmed. "I am still going to carry on street trading. I thought that prison was going to be bad, but I could 60 take it. It was the first rest I have had in four years, I put on half a stone in there."

Missed wet spell

His biggest regret was missing the wet spell with its healthy trade in umbrellas. He hopes that Westminster council will one day give him a licence to trade in Coventry Street, near the Trocadero, 70 where his father had a pitch.

"I enjoy my work. It's not just the money. I get pleasure out of it and the excitement of the street," he said. He was, however, reticent about disclosing his earnings. "I make a living," he said coyly.

Councillor Peter Hartley, chairman of Westminster 80 Council's Environment Committee, which has spent several hundred thousand pounds trying to rid the West End of unlicenced traders, said Jordan would be a "bloody fool" if he returned.

"We intend taking a Bill to Parliament with much stronger powers to deal with illegal 90 traders, including the seizure of their goods," he added.

Jailed umbrella man refused to fold up his brollies and go

A   Comprehension

Read the passage right through and then try to answer the following questions. Use your own words as far as possible.

1   What was unusual about Ronald Jordan being sent to prison?
2   In what way had he been punished in the past?
3   Why was he *greeted with a measure of resignation* by the magistrate? (lines 27–8)
4   Why did Ronald Jordan not mind being sent to prison?
5   What did he regret most about being in prison?
6   What is the meaning of *I make a living*? (lines 76–7)
7   Why do you think Ronald Jordan answered *coyly* (= shyly) when talking about his earnings?
8   Where in London is the *West End*? (lines 13–14)

B   Vocabulary

What is the meaning of the following words as they are used in the text?

1   *an undertaking* (line 4)   4   *reticent* (line 75)
2   *a snip* (line 38)   5   *to disclose* (line 75–6)
3   *brisk* (line 47)   6   *to rid* (line 83)

C   Writing Activity

A policeman confronts Ronald Jordan selling his umbrellas in the street, and accuses him of causing an obstruction. Write the dialogue that might take place between them.

D   Role-play

Act out the above situation in class. You may like some time to think about it and to make a few notes, but the role-play itself should be performed as spontaneously as possible, without any scripts.

Jailed umbrella man refused to fold up his brollies and go

This is quite a lively, and slightly unusual, piece about a determined and resilient street trader who is not afraid to break the law.

Note on the text
A *brolly* is an informal word in British English for an umbrella!

Warm-up

Ask students what they understand by a *street trader*. (Point out that in the UK you have to have a licence, granted by the local authority, to trade legally.) What kind of things do street traders sell? (Ask about students' own countries.) How can you tell (in Britain) if a street trader hasn't got a licence? (Always on the look-out for a policeman!) What would normally happen if someone was caught trading without a licence? (They would be fined.) Why are the authorities so strict? (Because of the obstructions that are caused to traffic and pedestrians.)

C   Writing Activity

Depending on the level of the class, the dialogue can be discussed together beforehand. There are many ways in which such an encounter can develop, but the following vocabulary and phrases may prove useful.

POLICEMAN: You're blocking the pavement/causing an obstruction/breaking the law; no-one can get by; it's dangerous; you've got to move; I'll give you x minutes to move; I'll have to arrest you; you're under arrest; I'm not concerned with y; I'm only concerned with (enforcing) the law.
RONALD JORDAN: I'm not doing anyone any harm; I'm not hurting/cheating anyone; I'm doing people a good turn; I'm selling them things they need; I'm providing a public service/doing an honest day's work; no-one's complaining; I have to earn a living; it's unfair; you don't interfere with other street traders; this is victimisation.

After their dialogues have been checked, students could read them in pairs, taking it in turns to play the parts of the policeman and Ronald Jordan (four 'readings' altogether!). If, however, there is time to do written work in class, students could work in pairs from the beginning, and produce one version between them.

Note
It is a good idea to have one or two 'demonstrations' from students to the whole class before beginning the simultaneous pair work. This gives an opportunity for the teacher to comment on general delivery and expression, as well as on intonation (particularly important in this dialogue) and the pronunciation of key words. With regard to intonation, students should be encouraged to decide beforehand the attitudes that both policeman and Ronald Jordan are going to adopt. The policeman could be conciliatory and reasonable and Ronald Jordan aggressive and stubborn, or vice versa. Or they could adopt similar attitudes.

D Role-play

This is an extension of the previous exercise and should be done without scripts.
Some people could take the part of customers, and a few umbrellas on a table would
add a little colour!

Sayings of the famous

1

I don't have a sugar problem; I don't have cholesterol trouble. I just have a calorie problem.

2

My life's work has been accomplished. I did all that I could.

3

Girls are a distraction and can easily cost points.

4

People are capable of doing an awful lot when they have no choice, and I had no choice. Courage is when you have choices.

5

I could go on stage and make a pizza and they'd still come to see me.

6

It's all to do with the training: you can do a lot if you're properly trained.

7

I have never experienced personally what racial prejudice is like, but I do understand prejudice. I do understand what it is like to be out of the mainstream of society.

8

I stopped going to see my films when I began to watch what was bad about my face, my neck, my body, my voice.

9

When a man opens the car door for his wife, it's either a new car or a new wife.

10

There is no such thing as Society. There are individual men and women and there are families.

11

People today are still living off the table scraps of the sixties. They are still being passed around – the music and the ideas.

12

It's just not worth the pain any more.

13

Will the Church succeed in becoming a promoter of true peace?

14

A woman should have a trim waist, a good 'up top' and enough down the bottom, but not too big.

15

I am not interested in fashion, only in creating good classic design.

16

Not long ago 541,000 people obeyed a single command I gave. Today it's even difficult to get a plumber to do what I want.

17

I've never been an intellectual, but I have this look.

18

I would walk miles for a bacon sandwich.

A   Matching Exercise

The eighteen sayings quoted on page 13 are all by well-known people. Read the sayings and then try to decide who said them, choosing from the list below.

Boris Becker
The Princess of Wales
Pope John Paul II
Katharine Hepburn
Lady Thatcher
Luciano Pavarotti
Bob Dylan
Queen Elizabeth II
Woody Allen

General Norman Schwarzkopf
Jimmy Connors
John Major
Prince Philip, Duke of Edinburgh
Frank Sinatra
Mikhail Gorbachov
The Duchess of York
Terry Anderson (former Beirut hostage)
Ferdinand Porsche

B   Speaking Activity

Choose one of the famous people listed and prepare a short talk to give to the class on his or her life or achievements. You may need to do some research in a library for this.

C   Writing Activity

Choose one of the famous people listed and write a brief 'pen portrait' of him or her. Again, you may need to do some research for this.

Sayings of the famous

This is a 'Friday afternoon' activity. If you think any of the names might be unfamiliar to your class, you could check with them and fill in any details or background before they begin the exercise.

The activity obviously lends itself to students working together in pairs or small groups, and you could make it into a competition.

GET TO WORK ON A SUMMER JOB

DYMPHNA BYRNE
reports on holiday work and leisure for young people

YOUNGSTERS planning inexpensive or working holidays should get to work now. According to Simon Godfrey, of York University's travel shop, students frequently miss good travel deals, particularly flights, by looking after, rather than before, exams.

10 Reliable working holidays – helping with fruit harvests, working in a hotel, on a campsite or on a dig – need paperwork. Every year there are horror stories of penniless youngsters turning up unannounced at French vineyards not being able to find work or accommodation and not having the 20 fare home. February is the time to get on with the letters of application for a guaranteed summer job.

The new editions of the invaluable annual guides for working holidays are out. 'Summer Jobs Abroad' and 'Summer Jobs in Britain' are published by a commercial 30 concern, Vacation Work Publications, 9 Park End St, Oxford, at £6.95 each from book shops. 'Working Holidays' £8.80 from bookshops is published by the Central Bureau, Seymour Mews House, Seymour Mews, London W1, a Government-funded charity.

All three guides have an 40 enormous range of jobs, paid and volunteer, with more emphasis on community and volunteer jobs in 'Working Holidays'. Also excellent value is 'Work Your Way Around the World' published by Vacation Work Publications, 9 Park End

Street, Oxford OX1 IH5. (£8.95 from bookshops.)

50 Conservation work – repairing dilapidated historic buildings, clearing overgrown land, rebuilding dry-stone walls, restoring canals or railways – is increasingly popular. You'll need plenty of energy and a tetanus shot. There's high job satisfaction but little or no pay.

To practise languages and 60 earn money abroad – about £80 a week – try courier work for a rent-a-tent company. Canvas Holidays, Eurocamp and Sunsites have tents in France, Germany, Switzerland and Italy. Preference is given to language students.

Hotel work is available in most European countries for 70 chamber maids, chalet girls, bar staff and waiters. Norwegian hotels pay well. All these jobs need a two- or three-month commitment.

Scaling cathedrals is a change from digging archaeological ditches. Cathedral Camps, for those between 17 and 25, has one-80 week cleaning and renovating programmes on such magnificent buildings as York, Ripon, Southwark or Bristol. Volunteers are asked for £25 towards board and lodging; some local education authorities help with expenses. Large s.a.e. to the information officer, Crow Hill, High Birstwith, 90 Harrogate HG3 2LG.

Youth hostelling is ideal for children planning their first holiday without parents. Our eldest was 14 when he cycled in the

Heart of England with friends. For parental peace of mind the hostels were booked and paid for beforehand and the boys rang home every night – all 100 hostels have pay telephones.

There are 5,000 hostels in Britain and abroad. Annual membership is between £1.90 and £8.30 depending on age – details from Membership Dept, YHA, Trevelyan House, 8 St Stephen's Hill, St Albans, Herts AL1 2DY. The handbook listing all the hostels in England and 110 Wales is £3.99 (there is also an International handbook at £6.55). 'Great Escapes in Britain', from the same address, has excellent adventure holidays for 10-year-olds upwards.

Cycling in Holland is a good first time abroad holiday for youngsters. This friendly country, where English is spoken 120 widely, looks kindly on cyclists and has good youth accommodation.

Cyclists in Britain planning to escape town by train need advance bicycle reservations on InterCity 125s, £3 a single journey. There are no charges or reservations on other services. The leaflet, 'The British Rail 130 Guide to Better Biking', is at stations. So are applications for Young Person's Railcards providing cheaper rates for 16 to 23-year-olds. Cost: £16. Also Inter-Rail cards, which give a month's unlimited travel for those under 26 in 24 European countries. Cost: £175.

Most European railways 140 have good deals for young people; tourist offices in Lon-

Read the article right through carefully and then test your memory by seeing how many of the following questions you can answer.

Grape-picking in France is hard work: make sure you arrange work and accommodation in advance.

don have details. For route planning get either BR's international passenger timetable or Thomas Cook's Continental timetable.

The National Express student coach card, £6 a year, gives a third off travel on
150 National buses. Student travel shops have details on other coaches, including those to the Continent and within the United States.

For parental peace of mind on accommodation, AJF – *Accueil des Jeunes en France*

– a non-profit-making organisation a little like the YMCA,
160 has offices at four Paris stations guaranteeing youth accommodation on arrival. It also has provincial accommodation in hostels, student halls of residence, budget hotels and international youth centres. Details from AJF, 12 rue des Barres, Paris 4e.

Full-time students from 14
170 upwards travel cheaper with an ISIC – International Student Identity Card – which gives air, rail and coach travel conces-

sions and discounts for theatres, museums and art galleries. The card, recognised worldwide, costs £5 annually – application forms from student travel offices or ISIC, PO Box
180 190, London WC1.

Companies specialising in student travel, STA Travel, Worldwide Student Travel and USIT, sell through university and college travel shops and the Student Travel shops in London and other major cities.

All have handbooks listing discounts and special offers.

Get to work on a summer job

A   Scanning Exercise

'Scanning' is looking through a text in order to find particular information. We scan, for example, when we look for a number in the telephone directory – we don't 'read' all the names and numbers on the page.

   Use the article about summer jobs for students as a scanning exercise. Look at the questions below and see how quickly you can find the answers – don't read the whole article at this stage.

1   In which country are hotel staff well paid?
2   How much does a Young Person's Railcard cost?
3   What is the minimum age you must be to go on a Cathedral Camp?
4   What kind of card do you need to get in order to obtain student concessions?
5   How much is the book *Working Holidays*?
6   In which city in Great Britain is the headquarters of the Youth Hostels Association?

7   What is the maximum age you can be to be eligible for an Inter-Rail Card?
8   How much can you earn a week as a courier for a camping company?
9   Which country welcomes cyclists?
10   In which city is *Working Your Way Around the World* published?
11   How much does it cost to take a bicycle by rail on an ordinary train in Great Britain?
12   Should you start looking for vacation work before or after the summer exams?

B   Vocabulary and Abbreviations

When you have checked your answers to Exercise A, read the article right through and then discuss with a partner the meaning of the following terms and abbreviations. In most cases the context should provide you with a clue.

1   *a dig* (line 13)
2   *board and lodging* (line 85)
3   *an s.a.e.* (line 88)
4   *the YHA* (line 106)

5   *an InterCity 125* (line 126)
6   *BR* (line 143)
7   *the YMCA* (line 159)

C   Talking Points

1   Which of the various summer jobs mentioned in the article specially appeals to you? Discuss with others in your group, giving reasons for your choice.

2   Make a list of all the advantages of doing a summer job. Then compare your list with a partner's or with those of others in your group.

D   Speaking Activity

Have you ever done a holiday job? If so, tell others about the experience – either informally or by preparing a brief talk for the class. Would you recommend this particular job to others?

E   Writing Activity

Now is the time to get on with the letters of application for a guaranteed summer job. Discuss with your teacher the layout and type of language needed for such a letter. Then, **either**

a   choose one of the organisations mentioned in the article and write a letter asking for further information or requesting a particular publication, **or**

b   choose a particular kind of job from among those mentioned in the article – for example, a courier or hotel work – and write a letter of application. This will have to be more detailed, as you will need to give some information about yourself, saying when you are available and what qualifications or experience you have. You will also need to ask for information about the job – hours of work, rates of pay, accommodation, etc. Invent a company's name and address to write to in order to be able to include it in your letter heading.

Get to work on a summer job

An article about the different kinds of summer jobs available to young people; the piece also contains suggestions for inexpensive ways of travelling, both in the UK and on the continent of Europe, as well as details of where to obtain current guides and handbooks.

Warm-up

Ask students if they have ever done a holiday job. What was the experience like? Invite one or two examples, but try not to let this stage go on for too long (see **D Speaking Activity**).

Headline

A play on words. *To get to work (on)* = to begin to do something.

A   Scanning Exercise

It is important that students do not see the passage before the scanning exercise, or it will lose its point (they may well then simply be using memory).
  There are a number of ways of approaching this exercise:

1   Make it into a class competition. Divide into two teams (no need to rearrange seating). The teacher reads out the questions (students shouldn't see them at all), the first person to call out the correct answer scoring a point for their team. Confirm the answer for the class, with the line reference, and let them find it before going on to the next question. Answers should come progressively more quickly as students become familiar with the text!
2   Let students see the questions and write down the answers. Either give a (strict!) time limit (ten minutes is about right) and collect in the papers, or make it a race, the first one with all twelve correct being the winner (collect up the papers in order of completion; the answers can easily and quickly be checked on the spot).
3   As Number 2, but students work in pairs, one doing the scanning and the other writing down the answers.

B   Vocabulary and Abbreviations

Check that students know how to pronounce the abbreviations correctly. Emphasise not just the correct letter names, but the length of vowel (full) and any necessary linking (not all run together!).

Example YMCA = /waɪjemsiːjeɪ/.

C   Talking Points

2   Obvious advantages include: money, helping the community, meeting other young people, travel, practising languages, learning to be independent, satisfaction from doing a useful job.

D   Speaking Activity

This could be done in pairs, the students exchanging holiday work experiences. To encourage listening (and clear speaking!) students could then be asked to report back to the class the job experiences of their partner.

E   Writing Activity

Some useful phrases when requesting information are:
I should be grateful if you could send me . . .
I should be glad to receive . . .
Could you also (possibly) send me/tell me/let me know . . .
I enclose a stamped addressed envelope.

Option **a** need only be the very briefest of letters. It can be used to teach (or revise) the layout of a formal letter, with appropriate salutations, signings off, etc. As neither personal names nor job titles are given in the addresses in the article, one has either to use *Dear Sirs*, which is very formal, or make up a suitable title, for example, 'The Editor, Vacation Work Publications,' etc., or 'The Director, Central Bureau,' etc., and then use *Dear Sir or Madam*. In each case, the ending will be *Yours faithfully*.

'Brain trains' give commuters chance to learn Japanese

By John Petty, Transport Correspondent

FLEETS of 'brain trains' on which commuters will be able to study anything from Japanese or palaeography to human biology, American football and antiques are planned by British Rail.

Some trains already have commuter study clubs, but Sir Robert Reid, BR chairman, is to give official backing to a huge expansion of the scheme.

10 And Mr Gordon Pettitt, general manager of Southern Region, said: "Every suitable train in the region is being surveyed to test demand for classes."

The commuter clubs started 10 years ago when Mr Michael Young, now Lord Young of Dartington, and his daughter,

20 Sophie, then 15, walked through a Cambridge–London train and questioned every passenger.

Huge range

They found many people interested in using their daily journey to study a huge range of subjects, such as psychology, architectural history, accountancy and law.

30 "The remarkable thing was that there were also people on the train willing to teach the same subjects at no charge," Lord Young said yesterday. "It was a kind of educational miracle."

Now the commuter clubs offer more than 100 classes a year, generally with three

40 pupils and one teacher in each group.

They are organised by Mrs Pamela le Pelley and her new assistant, Mrs Marilyn Phillips. Classes are usually free.

The main growth in the scheme will be in Network South East, because that is where long-distance commu-

50 ters are concentrated. But

Glasgow–Edinburgh is among other routes with study clubs.

Places saved

Surveys to extend the system are being carried out on trains from Salisbury, Portsmouth, Didcot, Dover, Bournemouth, Bognor and many other places.

British Rail provides stick-

60 ers to put on carriage windows and cards to put on seats to save places for the regular travelling students.

Learning Japanese has proved particularly attractive on trains bound for the City. A request for a class on American football has come from the Littlehampton line, while

70 human biology – with a different part of the body studied each week – is on the Didcot–Paddington line.

The request for a class on palaeography – the study of the history of handwriting – was on the Portsmouth–Waterloo line.

'Brain trains' give commuters chance to learn Japanese

A   Memory Test

Read the article right through carefully and then test your memory by seeing how many of the following questions you can answer.

1 What 'nickname' is given to those trains where passengers can study on their way to work?
2 How long ago did 'commuter clubs' start?
3 How much do the classes cost?
4 Where do the teachers come from?
5 How many students are there usually in a class?
6 In which part of Britain are the commuter clubs concentrated?
7 What are placed on carriage windows to reserve the compartments for 'student' passengers?
8 Which subject is popular with business people travelling to the City?
9 Which line in Scotland has trains with study clubs?
10 Several subjects for study that passengers were interested in were mentioned in the article. How many can you remember?

B   Talking Points

1   What do you think of the idea of a 'brain train'? Do you think that such a scheme would be practical or popular in your country?

2   If you were a commuter, travelling into a big city every day to go to work,
   a   what subject would you like to study?
   b   what subject would you like (and be able) to teach?

'Brain trains' give commuters chance to learn Japanese

This is a very straightforward piece and should be well within the ability of lower-intermediate students.

Warm-up

Ask students if they know what a *commuter* is. Why do people commute? (Too expensive to live in the city centre/prefer to live in the suburbs or the country.) What are the disadvantages of commuting? (Expensive, time-consuming, tiring.) Are there any possible advantages?

A Memory Test

Tell the class they are going to have a memory test and set a time limit for the reading – say four to five minutes. Avoid, if possible, any discussion of vocabulary at this stage – it is a distraction and, by focusing attention on a particular part of the text, tends to pre-empt and spoil the test! If students really need to, they could use a dictionary, though this takes up valuable reading time. Don't allow any note-taking!

The test itself may be a written one or it could be used as the basis for a team competition: students call out the answers, the first (correct!) one gaining a point for the team.

Cartoon

1

5

A BOY AND HIS DOG HIKING LIKE PERFECT COMRADES THROUGH THE WOODS

2

6

3

7

4

This **Peanuts** cartoon has become disarranged. By studying the pictures and reading the captions you should be able to put it back into its correct sequence. It's not difficult!

Cartoon

See General Note on page xii.

THE GREAT HURRICANE (1)

Houses damaged, cars wrecked, power cuts, no trains . . . the most ferocious storm for three hundred years did not spare anybody

Battle against the disaster in the night

SOUTHERN Britain was a scene of devastation when the dawn came after a night of howling terror and confusion. Meanwhile, the East Coast awoke to face the full fury of the storm.

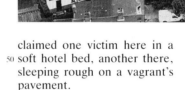

Across most of the south, there was no electricity, no transport, many roads closed and many telephones not working.

10 Not even the worst winter blizzard could have paralysed the country with such total efficiency.

Some people surveyed the damage: hundreds of cars destroyed by uprooted trees, thousands of windows smashed, roofs torn off, garages demolished.

20 Some people set out for work to find trees and lampposts across the roads. They abandoned cars to walk to railway stations – and there they found no staff and no trains.

Awesome

Some people – workers in the emergency services – went on doing what they had been doing all night, fighting flat out 30 to save their fellow citizens from the effects of a natural disaster greater than anything Britain had seen for 300 years.

To police headquarters in the different counties, the reports flooded in. They concerned deaths into double figures and injuries into the hundreds.

40 The storm had struck with awesome indifference to human frailty or strength, affluence or poverty.

Drivers of high-priced cars found them crushed and broken, side by side with old bangers equally destroyed.

Death struck impartially. It claimed one victim here in a 50 soft hotel bed, another there, sleeping rough on a vagrant's pavement.

It took young and old. People died in their homes, in their cars or doing their jobs in the battle against the storm's ravages.

In human terms, the storm broke down barriers and re-60 serve, bringing forth a flood of kindly neighbourliness.

In the worst-hit areas, thousands of people were up through the night, opening their homes to others who had lost theirs.

In the wrecked caravan parks of the South Coast, firemen and police waded through 70 deep water to rescue elderly retirees from mobile homes that were now piles of twisted metal and broken glass.

Hospitals could not telephone their staffs to man the additional emergency rooms that were needed.

The staffs fought the wind and the danger – and at the 80 peak of the storm it was very dangerous to take to the streets – to turn up voluntarily in their hundreds.

So did the part-time workers in the front line of emergency services, special constables, ambulance men, part-time firemen.

Two of these, from Christ-90 church, Dorset, Ernest Gregory, 47 and Graham White, 46, died when a tree crushed the cab of their fire engine. They were answering an emergency call.

Across the country, firemen broke into damaged buildings to save lives, to evacuate the old from risky tower blocks 100 and cut the injured out of smashed cars.

In the streets and on the motorways, the police worked frantically to divert traffic and clear blocked roads to prevent the havoc creating an even greater death toll.

This morning the storm, its power waning, is out in the 110 North Sea . . . and Britain begins a weekend of clearing up after a night to remember for a long, long time.

Battle against the disaster in the night

On the night of 15/16 October 1987, the south of England was hit by a hurricane. It was the worst storm Britain had experienced for 300 years. This article gives a general account of the damage caused and the work of the rescue services. The article in unit 12 gives a more detailed account of one man's experience of the Great Hurricane.

Vocabulary

There are a number of verbs in the present article which describe the violent action of the hurricane. Look at the two lists below and, after reading the article, see if you can match them up. You might like to do this with a partner. Try to do it without looking back at the text, and try to find the 'best' answer in each case.

the country was	damaged
trees were	blocked
windows were	crushed
roofs were	diverted
garages were	paralysed
cars were	evacuated
caravan parks were	uprooted
buildings were	torn off
the elderly were	smashed
roads were	demolished
traffic was	wrecked

When you have completed the list look back at the article to check your answers. Note that the past participles are sometimes used as adjectives in the text.

The Great Hurricane (1): Battle against the disaster in the night

An account of the night of 15/16 October 1987, when the south of England was hit by a hurricane.

Warm-up

To introduce this article (and the following one, which is linked to it), ask students what natural disasters they can think of. (Earthquakes, volcanoes, floods, typhoons, etc.) Have any of them ever experienced any? Which parts of the world are especially liable to such disasters? What famous volcanoes do they know? (Are they active or dormant?) Have there been any recent earthquakes or floods they can remember? Which members of society are especially important at such times? (Firefighters, ambulance workers (rescue services), the police, the army, voluntary workers, social services.) After initial rescue, what are the common needs of people caught up in such catastrophes? (Medical attention, food, shelter, clothing, money, personal counselling, etc.)

The passage itself is fairly straightforward, in short paragraphs and narrative in style and does not demand very much in the way of interpretation. However, teachers may like to check understanding of the following points:

1   What is the meaning of *Death struck impartially?* (Line 48: people died at random.)
2   What 'good' did the storm bring? (See lines 58–61: people offered help and showed kindness to their neighbours.)
3   In what way were the staffs of the emergency services particularly brave? (See lines 78–88: they ventured out into the streets, in order to report for work, at great personal risk.)

Make sure that students read the article before attempting the exercise! The meanings of the participles can be discussed in class in their context and then the exercise used as a test.

Five other past participles are used in the text to describe a state of damage to cars. Ask students to find them as a scanning exercise.

THE GREAT HURRICANE (2)

Nearest to nuclear war

Note: Sevenoaks is a town in Kent, in the south east of England, about 25 miles from London. It was one of the places most badly hit by the hurricane, and only one of its seven famous oak trees was left standing. Bruce Cova, the subject of this article, is the chief executive officer of Sevenoaks District Council.

Bruce Cova, untypical bureaucrat. 'They call me John Wayne.'

Mr Cova woke up one morning to find he had 900 miles of road to clear and only six experienced foresters. 'We took on anybody with a chain saw or a JCB. About 100 men in 20 gangs worked from dawn to dusk, from 9 a.m. Friday morning for nine continuous 10 days, fed by the WRVS. Thirty Royal Engineers came the next day with £1m-worth of equipment, for a fortnight. Trapped residents felt they'd been relieved by the cavalry.'

He hopes this is the nearest he will ever come to facing a nuclear war. 'We had no communications, no power and at 20 one stage, no petrol. When we run practice courses for the next war, we assume we'd send people out to get things done before the fall-out. The fact is you're not going to get anyone out there. There was only one way in or out of Sevenoaks for many days. It's pointless to talk about liaising 30 with the County or anyone else. The Army from Maidstone had a 20-mile detour to get here.'

If the storm had happened during the day, Mr Cova says there would have been thousands killed. 'Thank God,' he says, 'the Met men *didn't* know. Had they warned 40 us there would have been many dead. Folks would have gone to fetch Mum or move the car. The trees on either side of one of our main roads, Everlands, fell together, like two great hands, fingers interlocked, suspended 15 feet above the ground for two miles. And nobody died. 50 Saturday night would have been different.'

Tall and handsome, the bearded Mr Cova, blue jeans and Guernsey, isn't quite what one expects of a civil servant, chief exec at that. 'Bureaucracy's gone out of the window,' he says. 'We don't ask whose responsibility it is – if some- 60 one's got a tree through their roof and we've got a crane, we haul it out. We don't care if it's council or private. The council tip closed at 5 p.m. and refused to take branches. I told him I'd drive a truck through his gates if he didn't open up. They call me John Wayne.

'I sent a man from the Plan- 70 ning Office across the fields in his shorts to see if the 30 people trapped in St Julian's Commune were dead or alive. He climbed out of a pile of wood and said "Hello, I'm from the District Council, are you all right?" He was their first outside contact in three days. Maybe, for the first time, peo- 80 ple won't mind paying their rates. I hope they remember when it goes up.'

On 6 December at 11 a.m., Mr Cova hopes several thousand will witness the planting of seven young sessile oaks from the Forestry Commission, on The Vine cricket green at Sevenoaks. To swell 90 the funds of his appeal, Trees for the Future (TFTF), he'll be selling slices from the fallen past, the previous seven oaks of the town.

Nearest to nuclear war

A General Comprehension

Read the article right through and then try to answer the following general question. Choose the best answer.

Broadly speaking, the article is about:

1 The after-effects of a severe storm.

2 The way one man handled an emergency situation.

3 The importance of preparing for natural disasters.

B More Detailed Comprehension

1 *Trapped residents felt they'd been relieved by the cavalry* (lines 14–15). What is the speaker comparing the hurricane experience to?

2 In what way does Bruce Cova think that the disaster was similar to a nuclear war?

3 Why is Bruce Cova described as an *untypical bureaucrat*? (picture caption)

C Vocabulary

1 Find a single word in the text for each of the following:
  a a group of labourers
  b a period of two weeks
  c the opposite of a 'short cut'
  d a place to dump rubbish
  e a machine for lifting heavy objects

2 What is the meaning of the following verbs as they are used in the article?
  a *to take on* (lines 4–5)
  b *to liaise* (line 29)
  c *to haul* (line 62)
  d *to witness* (line 85)
  e *to swell* (line 89)

3 You may not have come across the following terms before, but can you guess what they mean from the context?
  a *a JCB* (line 6)
  b *the WRVS* (line 10)
  c *the Met men* (line 38)
  d *a Guernsey* (line 54)
  e *rates* (line 81)

D Grammar

Had they warned us, there would have been many dead (lines 39–41).
This is an alternative form to *If they had warned us . . .* and is quite common, especially in writing. Change the following sentences to the alternative form by placing the auxiliary verb *had* first. Remember, *if* is omitted.

1   If there had been more experienced foresters available, the work wouldn't have taken so long.

2   If the storm had happened during the day, there would have been thousands killed.

3   If the roads hadn't been blocked, the Army wouldn't have had to make a 20-mile detour.

4   If the men at the council tip hadn't opened the gates, Bruce Cova would have driven a truck through them.

E   Role-play

Imagine that Bruce Cova is to be interviewed in a radio magazine programme, two weeks after the storm struck. Divide into two groups. Those in one group prepare to play the part of Mr Cova, while the others prepare questions to ask him. Reporters may refer to their questions, but Mr Cova should answer without reference to the text. If you forget, be inventive!

The Great Hurricane (2): Nearest to nuclear war

This article about one man's experience of the Great Storm can be used as follow-up to the previous unit.

C Vocabulary

Please note Vocabulary Exercise C.3 before answering students' queries about what a JCB is!

Notes on Exercise C.3

JCB: Don't let students try to work out what the initials stand for – it could take all day! (It's a mechanical excavator named after J.C. Bamford, its manufacturer.) They should, however, be able to work out from the context that it's some kind of mechanical tool.

WRVS: Try to elicit the four words – the only difficult one might be *V* for *Voluntary*.

the Met men: *warned* (line 39) is the key word here.

Guernsey: the picture helps! Don't labour the word, though – it's not in common use.

rates: again, this should be possible to guess (something people pay – and who to? Who does the Planning Officer work for?)

Note: Since this article first appeared, rates have been abolished. They were replaced by the Community Charge (Poll Tax), which itself was replaced by the Council Tax in April 1993.

D Grammar

Note that *Hadn't* is not possible in this construction (numbers 3 and 4).

E Role-play

See General Note on page xiii.

Matching Titles: TV Programmes

These television programme 'blurbs' and their titles have become mixed up. Can you sort them out? By reading the information carefully you should be able to match up each one with its correct title.

The Natural World

Counting down the latest UK music charts is Jakki Brambles, the Radio 1 DJ who scooped the music world last year by flying to Los Angeles for an exclusive interview with megastar Madonna.

Director/Producer Stanley Appel

1

Singles

The live magazine show which covers the latest in technology, medicine and the environment. This week from Sweden, robot re-fuelling – the petrol pump that gives you four-star service. Simply drive up, slot in a credit card and let it do the rest. It finds your petrol tank, flips off the filler cap and delivers just the amount of petrol that you need – and all without you lifting a finger. And back in London, a look at Britain's newest, tallest skyscraper, the controversial Canary Wharf. Can this triumph of engineering convince disillusioned locals and a sceptical City that the future lies in the east? With Judith Hann, Kate Bellingham, Howard Stableford, John Diamond and Carmen Pryce.

Producer Richard Dale
Editor Dana Purvis

2

Food and Drink

Galaxy in Creation?
Astronomers have found what seems to be the most luminous object known in the universe. It is 16,000 million light years away and 306 million, million times brighter than the sun.
With Patrick Moore.

Producer Pieter Monsurgo

3

The Sky at Night

A five-part series about the origins of the computer.
2: *Inventing the Future*
Forty-five years ago a few brave souls risked everything to prove that computers were destined for more than just the laboratory. Narrated by Lesley Judd and Andrew Sachs.

Producer Nancy Linde
Series producer John Palfreman

4

Top of the Pops

Today, the *Bride of the Year* is selected from ten couples who were shortlisted from hundreds. Plus, frou-frou party frocks, gems and jewels. With Jeff Banks, Selina Scott and Caryn Franklin.

Producer Clare Stride
Executive producer Roger Casstles

5

The Dream Machine

A series in which artists talk about drawing. Roy Marsden works with a variety of media, combining rubbings, paint spray and line to produce his images. His series of pictures called *About the House* explores the shapes and surfaces of the home he has created for himself in Wales.

Producer Dick Foster

6

Making Their Mark

Monkeys on the Edge. The fast-disappearing Atlantic rainforest of Brazil is one of the most threatened landscapes on the planet. With its disappearance would go many rare and little-known animals and plants, and particularly primates. On the edge of extinction are South America's largest monkey – the dramatic muriqui – and one of its smallest – the strikingly beautiful golden lion tamarin. Will the international effort to save them be made in time?
Narrated by Rula Lenska.

Presentation Colin Cradock

7

Tomorrow's World

This week: families divided between meat eaters and vegetarians; a manifesto for healthy food; and a recipe for tender roast baby chicken. With Paul Heiney, Michael Barry, Jill Goolden and Oz Clarke.

Producers Alison Field and Tim Hincks
A Bazal production for BBCtv

8

The Clothes Show

Comedy series about lonely hearts written by Eric Chappell and Jean Warr, starring **Simon Cadell, Judy Loe**
Don't Look Now. Dennis is pursuing Pam, but what is he really after? With Eamon Boland and Susie Blake.

Director/Producer Graham Wetherell

9

Matching Titles: TV Programmes

Warm-up

You could discuss the kinds of TV programmes that are made and broadcast in different countries. Which are the most popular programmes? Which programmes do students like? How are TV companies financed? What part does the Government play in controlling/financing television? In the UK, is the BBC a state-controlled broadcasting service or an independent organisation? (Students often believe the former!) How is the BBC funded? (Through annual licence fees, payable by anyone owning (or renting) a television set – at present the fees are £26.50 for black and white, £80 for colour.) How many BBC channels are there? (Two – BBC 1 and BBC 2.) And independent channels? (Two – ITV (Independent Television) and Channel 4, which are financed mainly through advertising.) A number of satellite and cable channels are also now available to subscribers.

Why the stars of rock who sing of their pain might actually mean it

Annabel Ferriman
Health Correspondent

FORGET drink and drug abuse. Rock stars now face a new hazard – voice abuse, prompting 'safe singing' as the preoccupation of modern performers.

After last week's announcement that Genesis singer Phil Collins might give up touring
10 because live shows are wrecking his voice, doctors are counselling stars about the do's and don'ts of voice care.

'Pop singers facing trouble should be more selective about their work, should not smoke and should avoid smoky atmospheres,' said Mr
20 David Garfield Davies, consultant laryngologist at the Middlesex Hospital, London, who numbers many pop and rock stars among his clients.

'They should also rest their voice after a show instead of spending hours straining it at parties or chatting with fans. They should never take aspir-
30 in because that thins the blood and, if the singer coughs, this can result in bruising of the vocal chords,' he added.

Phil Collins, 41, who started a gruelling three-month 52-date tour of the US and Europe in May and who counts Princess Diana among
40 his fans, has admitted to using steroid drugs before some concerts to boost his voice.

But Mr Garfield Davies, who advises the National Theatre and the Royal Shakespeare Company, wonders whether Collins's trouble is due to steroids. 'Phil Collins is too experienced a singer to fall
50 into that trap. Some singers do rely on steroids, which are easily obtainable on the Con-

Phil Collins used steroids to help his stricken voice.

tinent. They are useful occasionally if a singer's vocal chords are inflamed and he has to go on stage that night. But they should not be taken regularly because they lead to a thinning of the voice muscle
60 in the long term.

'Phil Collins's problem is more likely to be over-use of his voice when younger. Most pop singers suffer from three things: lack of training, over-use and abuse of the voice.

'They have difficult lives. When they go on tour they do a vast number of concerts,
70 sing in smoke-laden places and then go off to the next gig in an air-conditioned bus or on a plane, both of which have low humidity, which is damaging to the vocal chords. They are expected to do three-month tours, which no opera singer would ever consider doing. They abuse
80 their voice by forcing it, so as to be heard over the background noise.'

Mr Garfield Davies, who is chairman of the British Association for Performing Arts Medicine, says rock and pop singers must also learn to warm up their voices before a

show and warm down after-
90 wards.

So whereas late parties, pill-popping and cigarettes used to be *de rigueur* for pop and rock stars, now a gentle warm-up before and straight home to cocoa and bed afterwards is recommended. So worried is the Association about the problems of singers
100 and musicians that it is setting up a telephone hotline to give advice to those needing help, particularly those away from home on tour.

It is also making training videos for GPs, one on musicians' problems, such as repetitive strain injury, and one on the voice. It has run nine
110 training sessions for doctors in the last two years. It has 300 doctors on its books and is setting up 12 specialist centres round the country where there are consultants with performing arts experience.

'It is impossible for musicians or performing artists to discuss their problems with a
120 colleague or friend in the profession, because once it is known that anyone has a ''problem'', their professional life is often finished. They are no longer booked by agents or fixers,' said Mr Garfield Davies. Other singing stars have suffered from serious voice problems. Elton John
130 and Lulu have had polyps removed from their vocal chords, and Tom Jones had problems including laryngitis and had to have his tonsils removed.

Equity, the actors' and singers' union, is also worried about the problem. Singer Miriam Stockley, vice-chair of
140 the concert and session singers' committee, said: 'What people forget is the amount of noise that you have to sing above.'

Why the stars of rock who sing of their pain might actually mean it

A   General Comprehension

1   In which two senses is the word *pain* used in the headline?

2   What does Mr Garfield Davies think is the cause of Phil Collins's difficulties?

3   What is the difference between *over-use* and *abuse* of the voice (lines 62/66)?

4   What positive things, according to the text, can help a singer to keep his or her voice in good condition?

5   What things should a singer try to avoid?

6   What action is the British Association of Performing Arts Medicine taking to help pop singers?

7   Why do singers tend not to discuss their voice problems with their colleagues?

B   Vocabulary

1   Which part of the body does a laryngologist (line 21) treat and what is the name of the medical condition associated with it?

2   Find another phrase for *so as to be* (lines 80–1).

3   *To warm up* (line 88) is a common expression, meaning 'to prepare oneself physically for a performance or activity'. *Warm down* (line 89) is not an everyday expression. What does the writer mean by it here?

4   What is a *telephone hotline* (line 101)?

5   What do you understand by *repetitive strain injury* (lines 107–8)?

6   What do you understand by the following words as they are used in the text?
    a   *a hazard* (line 3)   *e*   *to boost* (line 42)
    b   *a live show* (line 10)   *f*   *a gig* (line 71)
    c   *to wreck* (line 11)   *g*   *a GP* (line 106)
    d   *gruelling* (line 36)

C   Pronunciation

Does the word *cough* rhyme with
1   now?   3   stuff?
2   off?   4   no?

D   Writing Activity

Working in groups, design a poster for a pop singer's dressing room, drawing on the information contained in the article. Think of all the 'do's and don'ts' and present your message as powerfully as you can!

Why the stars of rock who sing of their pain might actually mean it

An article about the use and abuse of the voice by rock singers, with particular reference to Phil Collins of Genesis.

Warm-up

Not difficult! Ask students about their favourite pop singers. Do they know any 'old' pop stars? Who is the oldest one they know still singing? What possible health risks are pop singers often believed to be exposed to? What about the voice?

SOOTHE AWAY CARE

JAPAN'S strangeness doesn't hit you in the eye: it's tucked away in hidden corners and takes burrowing into. At first sight it appears overwhelmingly westernised, technologically light years ahead of the rest of us, famously efficient, an industrial nation of workaholics and brilliant copyists.

But beneath the modernisation, the Japanese are deeply rooted in their own traditions. One of the best ways to experience something of Japan's cultural traditions and hospitality is to stay at a ryokan.

Ryokan means inn in Japanese and they are all over the country, as variable in quality and price (dinner and breakfast are always included) as hotels anywhere. What differs is the degree of service, the setting and the food.

Sarah Drummond
washes off worry
while staying in
a traditional inn.

Ryokans have changed little over the centuries with the emphasis on both aesthetic appeal and physical comfort. At the top end of the market, kimonoed maids wait on guests hand and foot, sinking to the ground with immense grace, proffering trays, tea, towels, food with the traditional two-handed gesture and a bow, as I found when I accompanied my husband on a business trip.

Business completed, we went to Kyoto, the old capital, to visit temples and gardens. It's a three-hour train ride away (hot towels the moment you sit down, British Rail please note; Green Car is first class if you're really tired), passing vast stretches of industrialisation, Mount Fuji in the distance, tea plantations in the foreground.

In Kyoto we stayed at Sumiya Ryokan, a typically low two-storey old wooden building with rooms which look out on to several small gardens. Arriving at a ryokan, guests exchange their shoes for slippers; these are often too small for Europeans and induce a shuffling gait. The constant changing in and out of shoes and slippers or going barefoot in Japan soon becomes second nature, as it is *de rigueur* in temples, traditional restaurants and anywhere with tatami matting.

Interior of a modern ryokan

In your room (barefoot on the tatami), there is no bed, but a low table and legless chairs; in an alcove is a scroll or painting and by it an *ikebana* (flower arrangement).

There are shelves, a cupboard, sliding doors to divide the room; in a westernised ryokan (popular nowadays with affluent Japanese) there may be a telephone, a television, even an en-suite bathroom and a fridge packed with snacks and drinks.

After the maid has shown you in, she brings *ocha* (green tea) and biscuits and prepares a bath for you. Crisply folded *yukata* (cotton kimono-like garments, dark for men, pale for women) and *obos* (sashes) are provided for guests to use in the room and around the ryokan.

To European eyes the rooms seem bare though if you've been in Japan a few days you may already have tuned in to purity of line contrasting with the luxurious sense of being cosseted. It is also remarkably peaceful. At the entrance to the garden are *geta* (wooden clogs) for guests to wear outside.

Ryokans are popular in areas where there are hot springs, since bathing is an essential part of the stay. In some ryokans there are communal baths (one for men, one for women); in others they are private. In either case custom requires you to wash, and rinse, outside the bath (there may be a basin or bowls of water set aside for ablutions); only afterwards do you step into the wooden tub of very hot water that comes right up to your neck: it is extremely soothing.

Dinner is served in your room (you are by now clean, relaxed, robed, reclining on the legless chairs; the feeling of taking part in an amateur production of 'Madame Butterfly' has worn off).

Dish after dish of delectable food, exquisitely presented, is set before you, including pickled vegetables, raw fish, soup, rice, varieties of *tofu* (soya bean curd), *tempura* (fish and vegetables deep fried in a light batter), all in minute quantities. Japanese food is evidently the inspiration of nouvelle cuisine, though predating it by centuries. The idea is to savour small mouthfuls and not to be overstuffed. There is also *sake* (rice wine), and, afterwards, tea.

After the maid has cleared away, she moves the table aside and lays out the bed – a thick *futon* (sleeping mat), covered with sheets and quilted blankets. We substituted the brick-like Japanese pillows for cushions and slept soundly. I could not cope with Japanese breakfast (raw fish, rice and green tea), and chose continental instead.

■ Ryokans are best booked in advance, particularly in spring and autumn, when the Japanese travel in great numbers, including schoolchildren on sightseeing visits. From Britain contact ryokans through travel agents (they rarely have a telex). Ask for a room that looks on to a garden. The Japanese Tourist Office, at 167 Regent Street, London, W1 (071–734 9638), has a list of the country's top 350 ryokans, whose prices range from 10,000 yen to 60,000 yen a night (between £45 and £270). Tourist offices in Tokyo and Kyoto are a fund of information on ryokans; railway stations are a good source for finding more modest inns.

Soothe away care

A   Comprehension

Read the article right through and then try to answer the following (only four!) questions:

1   What is unusual for a Western person about the Japanese way of bathing?

2   Why did the writer not like Japanese pillows?

3   What is the meaning of the opening phrase: *Japan's strangeness doesn't hit you in the eye*?

4   The word *workaholic* (line 9) is a comparatively new, invented word, made out of *work* and *alcoholic*. What do you think it means?

B   Vocabulary

1   What is the meaning of the following words and phrases as they are used in the text?
   a   *tucked away* (lines 2–3)
   b   *shuffling gait* (line 61)
   c   *de rigueur* (lines 65–6)
   d   *to be cosseted* (line 100)
   e   *to recline* (line 124)

2   Find a word in the text with a meaning similar to each of the following:
   a   wealthy (page 31, column 1)
   b   relieving pain or tension (page 31, column 2)
   c   delicious (page 31, column 2)
   d   very small (page 31, column 2)
   e   to taste (page 31, column 2)

C   Speaking Activity

Make brief notes from the text about the characteristic features of a traditional Japanese ryokan and then, using just your notes, give a short talk to other members of the group, explaining what a ryokan is, and what it is like for the visitor to stay at one.

D   Writing Activity

Imagine that a friend of yours is planning to visit Japan, either on business or for a holiday. Write a letter, recommending him or her to stay at a ryokan at some time while visiting the country. Tell your friend what to expect and what surprises might await him or her.

Soothe away care

This piece looks a little dense on the page, but is really quite a good read, with plenty of interesting detail for the mind to focus on. You just have to get past the first sentence!

Warm-up

Ask students what they know about traditional Japanese life – they will probably know about the custom of bowing, the wearing of kimonos on special occasions, and might mention geisha girls! Do they know what a *ryokan* is? (Of course, if you have any Japanese students in the class, it's a good opportunity to get them to take over!)

C   Speaking Activity

This speaking activity can be shared around, by the teacher prompting various students to speak briefly about particular aspects of the ryokan, for example:

- the appearance and furnishing of the room (rather bare, shelves and cupboard, tatami mat, low table, legless chairs, no bed, flower arrangement and scroll or painting);
- what you have to wear (change into slippers or go barefoot, special cotton garments and sashes, and clogs for the garden);
- the tradition of bathing (washing before you get into the bath, and then bathing with the water up to your neck);
- eating (food served in your room – many dishes, beautiful presentation, small portions; rather special breakfast!);
- the service provided by the maid (brings you green tea and biscuits when you arrive, prepares your bath, lays out your special clothes, brings you dinner in your room, clears away afterwards and lays out your bed or *futon*).

D   Writing Activity

This is really a written follow-up to the above activity. Students should use the notes they made for that as a basis for their letter, and write in their own words. They must not copy out chunks from the text! (Prevent it, if you like, by depriving them of the books – withstand the howls of anguish.)

FISHY TALE THAT SPANS THE ATLANTIC

by Martin Bailey

1

He remembered that metal fish tags had been used for a promotion scheme during a fierce sales battle with the paper's rivals. Under the scheme, a number of trout in Grenadier Pond, in Toronto's High Park, were tagged – and anglers who succeeded in catching one were paid a $5 reward.

2

Mr McSween is determined to keep the tag – as a trophy over the malts in the Dunvegan bar. He is now patiently awaiting his cheque, which he plans to cash when the travelling bank pays its weekly visit to Dunvegan.

3

After receiving a phone call direct from the bar, the Canadian paper – equally puzzled – sought elucidation from 84-year-old Ralph Cowan, who had been its circulation manager in the 1930s.

4

It is, to be precise, a trout tag from Canada, dating from before the war. But how it got to the Western Isles, and why it took so long to do so, is a mystery which would have defied even Sir Compton Mackenzie's lively imagination.

5

IN THE best tradition of 'Whisky Galore,' Isle of Skye crofter Peter McSween has recovered a bit of flotsam from the foreshore which promises to keep him in single malts for a wee while yet.

6

The mystery is how the trout tag travelled nearly 3,000 miles to reappear on the Isle of Skye more than 50 years later. Mr Cowan can suggest only one explanation: 'Grenadier Pond is linked to Lake Ontario by a mile-long pipe and fish swim back and forth. One of the trout might have got into the lake and then been swallowed by a saltwater fish in the St Lawrence River. The bigger fish could then have crossed the Atlantic to Skye.'

7

Puzzled, Mr McSween and dog wandered into the Dunvegan Hotel bar, where fellow-drinkers decided that the *Star* must be a newspaper.

8

Despite the time-lag, the Toronto newspaper is honouring its commitment. 'A $5 reward at 1937 prices is now $43, which is on its way,' promised the *Star's* Gordon Barthos.

9

On a particularly windy afternoon two weeks ago, Mr McSween was walking his dog along the shore near Dunvegan when, he explains: 'I clambered behind a rock to light a cigarette and saw a small piece of metal lodged in a crack near the high-tide level. I had no idea what it was, but it was dated September 1937 and said that five dollars would be paid if it was returned to the *Toronto Star*.'

Fishy tale that spans the Atlantic

Jumbled Paragraphs

The paragraphs of this unusual story, about a fish tag that has just been found more than fifty years after being attached to the fish, have been jumbled up. Can you put them back into their correct sequence to tell the story? There are plenty of logical clues to guide you, and the first paragraph is quite easy to find!

Notes on the text

There are a number of references in paragraph 5 which might be unfamiliar to you.

1   *Whisky Galore* is a novel by Sir Compton Mackenzie (paragraph 4) – also made into a film, and based on a true story – about what happens when a ship carrying a cargo of whisky is wrecked off the shores of a Scottish island.
2   *The Isle of Skye* is the largest of the group of islands known as the Inner Hebrides, off the west coast of Scotland.
3   A *crofter* is a Scottish farmer.
4   *Flotsam* means goods from a wrecked ship, found floating on the sea.
5   A *single malt* means malt whisky – that is, not a blended variety.
6   *Wee* is a Scottish word meaning 'small' or 'little'.

Long-distance information: Peter McSween and the fish tag

Fishy tale that spans the Atlantic

A short piece in straightforward narrative style about the finding of a metal tag on the Isle of Skye, fifty years after it was attached to a trout in Toronto.

Warm-up

Geography lesson! If you have a map of the UK point out the islands of the Hebrides, both Inner and Outer, and pick out the Isle of Skye, the largest of the Inner group. You could talk a little about the life there – rural communities, chiefly relying on fishing and simple agriculture (crofting).

Then, if possible, show a world map, pointing out Toronto and Lake Ontario, and the fairly large expanse of ocean between Canada and the west coast of Scotland!

Headline

Ask students to look at the headline. What might the story be about? A fish that crosses the Atlantic? Point out the pun: a *fishy tale* is a strange or unusual story.

Jumbled Paragraphs

It is a good idea for students to work in pairs or small groups, as the exercise can stimulate argument and discussion. Encourage students to look for logical links – for example, personal pronouns (who or what do they refer to?) and the use of the definite article to refer back to something previously mentioned. Either point out, or go through, the notes to paragraph 5.

At the end, go through the correct sequence as a class activity, asking students to give their opinions as to the right order, and their reasons.

In theory, they should have looked up any unfamiliar words, so do a spot vocabulary check. A few words which might come up, depending on level, are: *trophy, puzzled, elucidation, to defy (the imagination), to clamber, to lodge.*

Memoirs of a secretary, or, as Miss Angell would put it . . .

(My life in shorthand)

Miss Angell: the perfect name for the perfect secretary

SHORTHAND emancipated Irene Angell. Three-quarters of a century ago, it gave her the means of surviving in a man's world.

Now in her nineties, Miss Angell still sends herself to sleep in her South London home thinking in shorthand and she can look back on a lifetime delineated in strokes and loops, hooks and dots.

Irene Angell was born in 1896, the year before Sir Isaac Pitman, inventor of the eponymous shorthand system, died. She has lived in six reigns and through two world wars.

Leaving school at 15, Irene attended the UK Secretarial College in Lavender Hill to learn shorthand and typing.

'You could either pay £5 and stay as long as necessary, or you could pay 15 shillings a quarter.'

Irene's parents could afford only 30 shillings. This financial handicap, she found, concentrated her mind wonderfully. 'I attended college on Mondays, Wednesdays and Fridays and I learnt shorthand and typing in six months.'

Off the cuff

Once qualified, she obtained a post in the City, where she worked for 10 shillings a week. Her office was situated in the old Wool Exchange, which is now the site of the Chase Manhattan Bank. 'I loved the old City with all its little courtyards,' she recalled, 'but that's all gone now.'

Miss Angell admires at least one thing about today's secretaries. 'They dress so beautifully,' she said. In her early days, office uniform was a long navy-blue skirt and a white blouse. If you were daring, you might wear a pink blouse, she recalled.

To keep their sleeves clean, secretaries wore paper cuffs, which they changed each day and on which they would often jot shorthand notes. Hats were *de rigueur* – felt in winter and straw in summer – but lipstick was forbidden. 'Not that I would have worn it,' Miss Angell said.

Working conditions were

terrible. Hours on weekdays were from 9 a.m. till 6 p.m. and on Saturdays 9 a.m. till 1 p.m. If the hours were long, the money was short. The return tram fare from Wandsworth to Southwark Bridge was three-pence a day and with lunch – steak and kidney pie, potatoes and a cup of tea – at sixpence, the young secretary was left with —?— a week*. After giving her mother five shillings for board and keep she retained precious little for her labours.

So good was Irene Angell's shorthand at interviews that prospective employers never bothered to take up her references. Her 120 words a minute won her several diplomas, a volume of Tennyson's poetry and 'Vanity Fair.'

'I loved Pitman's from the moment I saw it,' Miss Angell recalled. 'You've got to love it to mop it up.' Efforts to simplify the system do not meet with her approval. 'It may be easier to put it down, but it's not easier to read it back,' she said. 'What's the use of saving time putting it down, if you then spend four hours puzzling over deciphering it?'

Time was a luxury not to be squandered in young Irene's day. In one office where she worked, about 50 secretaries sat in a large room watched over by a supervisor. 'The supervisor would call you in and tell you your boss had rung,' Miss Angell recalled. 'When you went out and when you returned, you entered the times on a large board hanging on the wall and added in brackets the number of letters you had taken.'

Sack me, please

Machines are anathema to Irene Angell. Today she will not have a television set in her Clapham home and she tolerated the typewriter only because it enabled her to pursue her beloved shorthand. When dictaphones were first introduced she knew they would not catch on, she said, and when a firm where she was working adopted audio typing, she went to the boss and said he would have to sack her.

The boss did no such thing and Irene Angell continued working as a secretary until she was 82. Even then her addiction to Pitman's would not allow her to kick the shorthand habit and she continued giving private lessons to the children of neighbours.

One Victorian value this lively nonagenarian retains is her preference for a male boss. 'Once you put a woman in charge, she becomes autocratic and unbearable,' she warned. 'Look at Maggie Thatcher.'

Alan Road

*See question B.2

Memoirs of a secretary . . .

A   General Comprehension

Read the article right through and then try to answer the following questions.
1   What, in your own words, is *shorthand*?
2   Miss Angell's parents were quite poor, but how did this help her?
3   What do you understand by *board and keep* (line 78)
4   Why does Miss Angell not approve of simplified systems of shorthand?
5   What objection do you think Miss Angell had to dictaphones?
6   By using the word *addiction* in line 133 and the phrase *kick the habit* in lines 134–5, what does the writer compare Irene Angell's love of shorthand to?

B   Mathematical Questions

In 'old' money (pre 1971) there were 12 pence in a shilling and 20 shillings in a pound. Today there are 100 (new) pence in a pound. Can you work out the following and then convert the answers into modern currency?
1   How much did Irene Angell's shorthand and typing course cost altogether?

2   What is the missing figure in line 76?

3   If you assume a lunch break of one hour, how much an hour did Irene Angell earn?

4   How much personal spending money did she have a week?

C   Kings and Queens

Irene Angell has lived in six reigns (line 17). Can you name the six kings and queens?

D   Vocabulary

What is the meaning of the following words as they are used in the article?

1   *to emancipate* (line 1)
2   *daring* (line 51)
3   *to jot* (line 58)
4   *de rigueur* (line 59)
5   *precious little* (line 79)

6   *to mop (something) up* (line 91)
7   *to decipher* (line 99)
8   *to squander* (line 101)
9   *anathema* (line 115)
10   *to catch on* (line 124)

E   Role-play: interview

Imagine a reporter has been sent to interview Irene Angell on her 90th birthday. Divide into reporters and interviewees and prepare the role-play as guided by your teacher.

Memoirs of a secretary . . .

This is a straightforward piece, with not too much difficult vocabulary. It contains interesting revelations about life for a working woman at the beginning of the century and is written in an easy, flowing style, with a number of passages of direct speech.

Warm-up

As an introduction, ask students how they think the life of a secretary has changed in the course of the last 60 or 70 years. Guide them towards: working hours; pay; relationship with the boss; style of dress; introduction of mechanical aids – dictaphone, word processor.

Talk about shorthand. What systems do students know about? Are they familiar with any particular one? Is shorthand now completely out of date? (It is still used regularly in Law Courts, so that the judge can have immediate reference to something said earlier in the trial.) Would a system of shorthand be useful for study purposes, for taking notes at lectures? What special short forms of their own have students devised to make note-taking easier? What is the most important aspect of any shorthand system? (Being able to read it back!)

B Mathematical Questions

The answers to the mathematical questions reveal as much about social change as about 'old money'! It's quite useful for students to have some idea about 'pounds, shillings and pence', even today, as the terms often occur in literature.

C Kings and Queens

This exercise provides a good opportunity for a visit to the library! The students could come back with a list of dates as well.

E Role-play

See General Note on page xiii.

Matching Headlines

Here are nine more news stories, each of which should have a two-word headline – a word from Group A followed by a word from Group B. Study the news stories and then write the appropriate headline above each one.

A

SAILOR
JUNIOR
KNOCKED
SEA
MISERY
SOCCER
NICE
BOMB
PLANE

B

RESCUE
OUT
CACHE
WORK
ROBBERS
ENDS
SAFE
DEATHS
PROTEST

Three Britons are believed to have been among six passengers and crew killed when a light aircraft crashed off Antigua in the Caribbean.

1

Three thousand West Ham fans invaded the club's Upton Park pitch after a 1–1 draw with Wimbledon, and called for the board to be sacked. The fans are unhappy with the performance of the team and a controversial fund-raising plan.

2

Police seized nearly 3,000 lbs of explosives in a horsebox in Co. Antrim after IRA man Finbar McKenna died in a bomb blast near a Belfast RUC station.

3

Yachtsman Ron Taylor, 45, of Liverpool, was rescued after spending seven hours in a liferaft off the Cornish coast.

4

Police were yesterday seeking two boys, aged about 9 and 12, who stole £10,000 from an 80-year-old woman in Glastonbury, Somerset.

5

RAF helicopters rescued eight fishermen whose trawler caught fire off Caithness.

6

Professional boxing was banned at council-owned venues in Hackney, East London, a traditional stronghold of the sport.

7

Dublin police station charlady Bernadette Lynch, 60, won £225,000 in the Republic's state lottery – and vowed not to give up the job she loves.

8

Coach drivers in Majorca yesterday ended a strike over pay which had left thousands of British tourists stranded at the island's hotels and airport.

9

Matching Headlines

See General Note on page xii.

Notes on the text

Paragraph 3 – the *IRA* is the Irish Republican Army.

              – the *RUC* is the Royal Ulster Constabulary – the police force of Northern Ireland.

Paragraph 4 – the *Cornish coast* is the coast of Cornwall, a county in the south-west of England.

Paragraph 6 – the *RAF* is the Royal Air Force.

On foot to the roof of the world

Nepal: shrines, sacrifice, and a million-step stairway to majestic mountain peaks

by Andrew Morgan

TO STAND on top of Poon Hill on the rim of the Himalayas at dawn is a haunting and ▇1▇ experience.

Although it takes several days' hard trekking through West Nepal to reach this peak, at 10,600 feet Poon Hill seems very ▇2▇ when compared to the awesome mountains in the distance.

As the sun comes up the snow on the far peaks, mostly over 26,000 feet, takes on a thousand shades of light and dark. When the heat increases, blizzards of snow begin to whip up on them while the great ice-walls exude their impenetrable grandeur.

The mountains are so huge they seem just a pebble's throw away; in fact they are up to 20 miles distant.

Annapurna 1, at 26,545 feet, is the largest, towering like a white fist. Others, twisted and torn with ice, are even more dramatic. During a three-week trek in Nepal, the people and villages in the foreground may change constantly, but these mountains form a constant backdrop like wild old friends.

▇3▇ peaks are found in all directions from the capital, Kathmandu. To the northeast is the Everest range; to the west the equally ▇4▇ Annapurna massif. Expeditions for both mountains and the lower hills often start from the ▇5▇ town of Pokhara. The lake to the west, Phewa Tal, is in a time warp: a latter-day hippie stronghold where middle-aged couples wear Afghan coats, smoke grass and listen to Leonard Cohen.

My two-week trek was with Exodus Expeditions, based in London, who organise trips all over the world. There were 15 in our group, including a pair of fit Dutch pensioners, a Lan-

The village of Namche-Bazar, in the Himalayas

caster postman and his wife and a range of young professionals, mostly, it seemed, with scientific backgrounds.

This was the shortest Exodus trip, with the nights spent in tea houses rather than under canvas. As the monsoon was late in finishing, this was ███ 6 ███ , even though the inns were a touch ███ 7 ███ .

The Nepalese cook over wood fires, mostly with great expertise. Three-course meals of soup, vegetable hash and chocolate pudding would often appear within minutes.

The basic trek costs £1030, but that price can soon increase. Exodus hires out trek packs for the ill-equipped for £40. They contain ███ 8 ███ items such as a sleeping bag, duvet jacket, foam mat, water bottle and cape.

Some trekkers borrow equipment and this is better as some items in Nepal are not so clean. Other extras, particularly medicines, can also bump up the price.

AT Pokhara we stayed near a camp for Tibetan refugees. There are 12,000 in Nepal, families of those who fled the Chinese in the 50s. They brought carpet-making expertise with them and lines of young girls sit in the camp expertly making material that sells at outrageously low prices.

Setting off on the first morning was ███ 9 ███ because it was fine. Other days the ███ 10 ███

monsoon meant tramping through a downpour, frustrated by solid mist. It was not much fun and it is vital to get the timing right.

What we saw on that first morning summed up the Himalayan experience: ███ 11 ███ Nepalese working on simple, subsistence activities; dashing streams and fertile fields, all set against the hard mountain magnificence; and the ███ 12 ███ ceremonies for the Hindu new year.

For one, a group of men tethered a bullock and cut its throat on the village street. A crowd watched the creature's blood flood into a bucket before it choked to death. Nepal can be tough on western eyes.

On the lower slopes, Nepal seems like a million-step stairway to heaven. Some tracks follow river scree, but the paths are mainly steps made from the stones on the ground. This means a rapid rise in altitude and legs can suffer.

Exodus warn of the need to be fit and this should not be ignored. One day I climbed too rapidly and paid the price with painful knees on the descent.

OUR guides were ███ 13 ███ but not startling. Better ones can be hired in Kathmandu. For a few pounds a week they will carry packs, cook meals and be informative.

Of course Nepal is much more than just a series of

majestic peaks. It is a remarkable country in which Buddhist and Hindu religions live side by side. Shrines testify to the Kathmandu valley's role as a centre of pilgrimage, and the prayer wheels at Swayambhunath at Bodhnath are wonderful, belonging to sacred sites set up more than 2,500 years ago.

In all, there are about 30 ethnic groups in the valley. Many are in Kathmandu city and the adjoining Patan, as well as the remarkable Bhaktapur, which contains some of the valley's architecture. But it is the religious sites which are most ███ 14 ███ .

At Pashupatinath, a centre where Shiva is worshipped as a phallus, human cremations are common next to the temple built in 1696.

Further away from Kathmandu is the shrine at Dakshinkali, where animals like buffaloes and chickens are sacrificed twice a week. It is a ███ 15 ███ tourist site for those keen to record butchers standing ankle-deep in blood.

But it is the views from the peaks after a day's trek which are truly memorable.

To stand on the roof of the world and look down is a rare and wonderful event.

● *Exodus Expeditions are at 9 Weir Road, London SW12 0LT (081–673 0859).*

On foot to the roof of the world

A Vocabulary

First, read the article right through to get a general idea of what it's about. Don't worry about any new or difficult words, and ignore the gaps at this stage – you should still be able to get a good idea of the piece and capture the atmosphere. Then, after discussing with your teacher the meaning of the adjectives printed below, find their right place in the text. If working unassisted, remember to use a good English–English dictionary to check the meaning of any unfamiliar words.

1	handsome	6	crucial	11	popular
2	remote	7	majestic	12	lingering
3	adequate	8	evocative	13	humbling
4	demanding	9	seedy	14	insignificant
5	religious	10	memorable	15	fortuitous

B Pronunciation

Now put the fifteen adjectives into columns according to their stress patterns.

2-syllable words	3-syllable words	4-syllable words
— • • —	— • • • — •	— • • • • — • •

There is one 5-syllable word. What is it, and where is the main stress?

On foot to the roof of the world

An account of a trekking holiday in Nepal, with descriptions of both the country and its people.

Warm-up

A suitable lead-in to this travel piece is to ask the name of the highest mountain in the world. Which country is it in? (Nepal.) What mountain range does it belong to? (The Himalayas – two schools of thought about the pronunciation!) Do you know the names of any other mountains in the range? (Students may have heard of K2 and Annapurna.) Would you like to go there? (Maybe some have been already!) Is it necessary to be a mountaineer? Elicit the idea of *trekking*.

A Vocabulary

Discuss the meaning of the adjectives before beginning the exercise, students making notes about any that are new to them. Although one or two adjectives may seem difficult to fit in at first, each has its place according to meaning, context and 'rules' of collocation. None are really interchangeable. If students have difficulty with number 10, refer them to the earlier mention of the monsoon in line 64. When doing the exercise, it is a good idea for students to write out numbers 1 to 15 in their notebooks and write the correct adjective against each number, rather than, say, pencil in the numbers against the printed adjectives. This not only helps the learning of any new words, but also makes discussing the correct version much simpler later on.

This exercise could obviously be done as homework, but it also lends itself to pair work in class. As well as giving an opportunity for students to discuss words and their context, it gives the teacher a chance both to monitor students' work and to answer, informally, any general vocabulary questions about the text.

Please note that the size of each gap is not always an indication of the length of the missing word.

Note

The first 50 lines of this piece are rather heavily descriptive and some students might have difficulty getting into it. Begin, for all but advanced students, at line 51, *My two-week trek with Exodus Expeditions . . .* , where the writing becomes much more concrete and narrative in style. Students can then tackle the more demanding opening paragraphs once they have a good idea of the piece.

Note that the address of Exodus Expeditions is given. Why not get a student to write off for a brochure?

Chairborne aces of the hard court

ALAN ROAD meets the tennis players who are undaunted
by physical disability

WHEN Janet McMorran broke her back 12 years ago, the thing that rankled perhaps more than anything was the realisation that she would no longer be able to play tennis. The game had been a passion since childhood. 'I started playing when I was nine and I can hardly remember a time when I didn't enjoy it.'

It was a matter for further frustration when her children, Donald and Rowly, were born that she would never be able to face them across the net. 'I could swim with them,' she said, 'but I did not think I could play tennis.'

Then last summer she was in hospital in Stoke Mandeville when the International Games were taking place. She watched an exhibition of wheelchair tennis and responded when urged to have a go. It was a revelation.

On her brother's grass court, she had found it impracticable to propel a wheelchair, but a hard court was quite a different matter, she realised. The other discovery was the two-bounce rule, which for chairborne players makes the impossible merely implausible.

Now Janet is a member of the London Wheelchair Tennis Association and plays most Sunday mornings and occasionally in the week at Bishop's Park in Fulham. When three-and-a-half-year-old Donald and 18-month-old Rowly are old enough to hold a racket, their mother should be ready for them.

Wheelchair tennis is the brainchild of Brad Parkes, an American acrobatic skier who broke his back in 1976 and spent six months during his convalescence at international tennis centres.

Today there are 300 handicapped players in Los Angeles alone. The sport has been recognised by the world wheelchair games and is now established as one of the events at the Paralympic Games.

Apart from the two-bounce dispensation and the fact that players are permitted to 'foot-fault' with the front wheels of their chairs, LTA rules are adhered to. The chair is reckoned to be an extension of a player's body and so if it is struck by an opponent's shot the point goes to him.

What Chris Illingworth likes about the game is the fact that, unlike so many other wheelchair activities, you are classified not according to your physical disability, but according to your sporting ability. This, he feels, means that he can find his true sporting level among his fellow players.

When British Caledonian came up with a couple of free transatlantic air tickets last year, he and a colleague competed at the American open championships in Los Angeles with more than 300 handicapped players from around the world. They were soundly beaten in the doubles by French and Dutch pairs, but learnt a great deal from watching the likes of Brad Parkes.

The London club, which has half a dozen regulars and about the same number of occasional players, grew out of the determination of one young man – Simon Hatt. The 22-year-old arts administrator, who has been in a wheelchair ever since a childhood illness, badgered professional coaches at the Fulham park to knock up with him.

One of them, Gordon Gibbins, conceded that the wheelchair player's innate ability quashed any patronising tendencies he might have had. 'He was soon making passing shots and I thought "Let's stop being silly and start teaching the game seriously."' Gibbins is now responsible for all club coaching.

Simon Hatt's enthusiasm was infectious. Fellow wheelchair basketball players, Tony Holland, Noel McShane and Anthony Peterken were attracted to the summer sport and last year the club was started.

In their second season all the players are improving, but they would be the first to concede that their current game leaves plenty of room for that eventuality.

Sunday morning bystanders are surprised by the power of their shots, but as yet long rallies are a rarity. Players tend to hug the baseline, which gives them more time to make their shots. 'Sitting in a wheelchair, you can easily get lobbed,' Noel McShane explained.

The squeamish might find it somehow sneaky to place a shot deliberately out of the reach of a handicapped person – rather like taking a blind man to the middle of the road and abandoning him.

Wheelchair players have no time for such qualms. 'That's the idea of the game,' McShane said cheerfully. 'They are trying to do the same thing to you.'

For handicapped players like him, the use of a chair becomes intuitive. 'You don't think about moving your chair any more than an able-bodied player thinks about moving his legs.'

Which is not to say that a wheelchair is not important. Sports chairs are light, mobile and made to measure. More to the point, they can cost between £1,000 and £3,000 and 170 they are not available through the NHS.

Thanks to the generosity of Sealink and the Fulham and Hammersmith parks department, who are lending a minibus, a driver and Gordon Gibbins, club members are competing later this month at tournaments in France and 180 West Germany.

'It will be an opportunity to see how far they are behind,' said Gibbins. 'But then we are at tennis in general,' he added wryly.

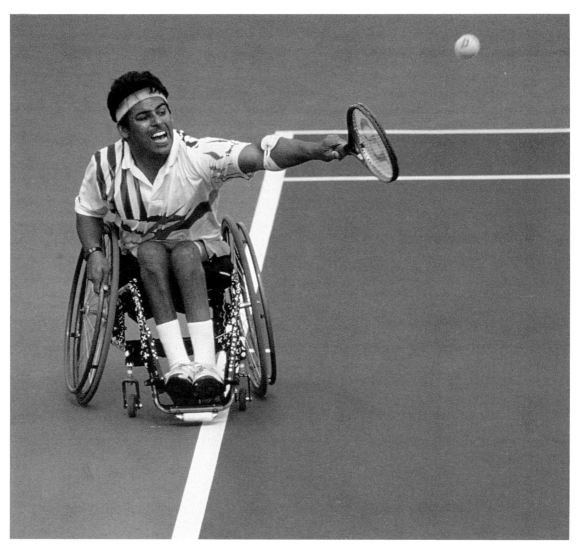

Fast service on wheels: a wheelchair player demonstrates his technique.

Chairborne aces of the hard court

Notes on the text

1   The LTA (line 68) is the Lawn Tennis Association.
2   The NHS (line 171) is the National Health Service.

A   Comprehension

Read the article right through and then try to answer the following questions.

1   What upset Janet McMorran when her children were born?

2   What is the special rule that makes playing tennis in a wheelchair practicable?

3   Who wins the point if a ball strikes the wheelchair – the striker of the ball or the person receiving it?

4   What was it that made Gordon Gibbins decide to teach wheelchair players seriously?

5   Why do wheelchair players usually play from the baseline? (two reasons).

6   How do wheelchair players feel about opponents who deliberately place the ball out of reach?

B   Vocabulary

1   Choose the best meaning for each of the following words, according to the way they are used in the text.

a   *undaunted* (headline)   *1* tested
                             2 not afraid
                             3 made nervous

b   *to rankle* (line 3)   *1* to surprise
                           2 to upset
                           3 to cause bitterness

c   *to adhere to* (line 68)   *1* to break
                               2 to change
                               3 to stick to

d   *to badger* (line 105)   *1* to ask persistently
                             2 to force
                             3 to bribe

e   *to quash* (line 111)   *1* to reinforce
                            2 to cancel
                            3 to change

f   *sneaky* (line 144)   *1* unkind
                          2 cruel
                          3 unfair

2   Find a word or phrase in the passage with a similar meaning to each of the following:

a   a brilliant idea (page 42, column 1)
b   a period of recovery after illness or an accident (page 42, column 1)
c   to play a game, such as tennis, but without scoring (page 42, column 2)
d   teaching a sport (page 42, column 3)
e   moral doubts or uncertainties (page 42, column 3)
f   natural, without thinking (page 42, column 3)

C Negative Prefixes

Notice the negative prefix *im–* in the words *impracticable, impossible* and *implausible* in the fourth paragraph. Can you make the following words negative by adding an appropriate prefix? (Be careful with double letters – do you know the rule?)

partial	offensive	responsible
musical	numerate	sincere
legible	mortal	manageable
religious	sophisticated	literate
necessary	hospitable	natural

D Numbers

You probably know that *half a dozen* (line 98) means *six*, but do you know how many the following are?

1 a score
2 a gross
3 a baker's dozen

Chairborne aces of the hard court

An article about how disabled people are able to play tennis and the success they have had.

Warm-up

Ask students if they know anything about sports for the disabled. They may have seen the special Olympics for the disabled on television. What sports can be played from a wheelchair? Basketball? Table tennis? Tennis? How might the rules have to be changed to make it possible to play tennis sitting in a wheelchair? (See section A, question 2.)

Headline

A pun on the word *ace*.

Quiz 1

The following questions are all based on the first twenty units of the book. See how quickly you can find the answers. If you have covered all the units, it shouldn't be too difficult to identify the articles – you may even know some of the answers from memory! If not, you may be able to get a clue to the relevant article from glancing down the Contents list at the beginning of the book.

1 Who is the chairman of Kentucky Fried Chicken?

2 Why might Phil Collins give up touring?

3 What is the basic cost of a trekking holiday in Nepal with Exodus Expeditions?

4 Who referees rugby matches on Saturdays?

5 How many sheep in Wales are still affected by radiation from the Chernobyl disaster?

6 What is the minimum cost of a sports wheelchair?

7 How much would you have to pay to go on a Cathedral Camp for a week?

8 In which year was Sir Isaac Pitman born?

9 When shouldn't you eat a heavy meal?

10 What is the name of Britain's tallest skyscraper?

11 How much does a National Express student coach card cost?

12 What is the address of the Japanese tourist office in London?

13 Who smokes 40 cigarettes a day?

14 How high is Annapurna I?

15 Who is the chairman of British Rail?

16 How much can you buy an umbrella for from a London street trader?

17 What is the address of Vacation Work Publications?

18 How many miles from London is Sevenoaks?

19 How much did Bernadette Lynch win in the Irish state lottery?

20 Who likes walking through the woods?

QUIZ 1 (TN)

Suggestions for using the Quiz

See General Note on page xii.

1   Students complete the quiz individually, writing down their answers. The first with an all-correct solution wins. (Collect papers in order of completion; the answers are very short, and easy to mark on the spot.)

2   As above, but students work in pairs.

3   Divide the class into two or more groups, and read out the questions in turn. Students call out the answers as soon as they find them (or, possibly, remember them!), the first correct answer scoring two points for the team. Deduct a point for any incorrect answer called out (this discourages wild guessing!). Students should have their books open at the Contents page – not the Quiz page!

TRIUMPH OF KIDNAP JENNY

by STEWART PAYNE and JENNY REES in Dublin

JENNIFER Guinness told last night how a mixture of anger and determination kept her going during her eight-day kidnap ordeal.

And it became clear that it was her remarkable courage in the last desperate hours which saved her life.

"What helped me through was a conviction that they were not going to get to me", said Mrs Guinness just hours after she was freed.

"I had no doubt that much of the time my life was in danger.

"But I couldn't afford to let myself lose hope. I was going to come out mentally and physically intact."

Mrs Guinness, 48, showed no signs of exhaustion as she joked with her husband, merchant banker John Guinness, 51.

She said that she told her abductors their ransom demand of £2 million was "crazy". When Mr Guinness was asked whether he ever had any intention of paying the ransom he replied firmly: "No".

Mrs Guinness, feigning mock anger, nudged him and said: "I hope you were, surely!"

She confirmed that the kidnappers originally intended to snatch her 23-year-old daughter Gillian. But she persuaded them to take her instead. "I suppose I pleaded with them that I would be much better. John would pay more for me," she said with a grin. But despite her easygoing manner, it was clear that for much of the time she suffered great discomfort.

Each time the kidnappers changed base she was bundled into the boot of a car. At other times she was tied up with masking tape stuck over her eyes.

She was determined, she

'I could not dare to give up hope'

said, to make a nuisance of herself. "It made me feel better."

She added: "My reputation, thanks to the newspapers, was of a strong woman. I'm sure they were very pleased to see the back of me."

But it was in the final hours of her ordeal that Mrs Guin-ness showed the most astonishing bravery.

The panicking kidnappers, surrounded by armed police, held a gun to her head and threatened to blow her head off. Yet Mrs Guinness remained calm.

With armed police surrounding the kidnappers in a flat in Dublin, they became jumpy. But she calmly reasoned with them, pointing out the futility of their position and gently persuading them that they had no choice but to give themselves up.

Mrs Guinness told them that to take her life could only make matters worse for them.

Her softly-softly approach paid off. At first light yester-

day the two remaining kidnappers walked from the flat
90 in the Ballsbridge district of
Dublin with their hands up
and surrendered.

Mrs Guinness was free. The
prayers of her family had been
answered.

The breakthrough in the
hunt came when police spot-
ted two known criminals driving a hired car which finally
100 led them to the gang's lair.

Swooped

On Tuesday evening they
swooped on a luxury home in
the suburb of Rathfarnam. It
was empty but they were con-
vinced that Mrs Guinness had
been there.

The action rapidly moved to
Waterloo Road in Ballsbridge.
Just after midnight police
110 found the hired car parked
outside No. 51.

Five minutes later one of
the kidnappers, named as
Tony Kelly, was seen leaving
the house. He began firing at
police. They returned fire and
Kelly was overpowered.

One of the gunmen came to
a window and shouted:
120 "We've got her inside. You
had better back off or we will
blow her head off."

Police then retreated and a
trained negotiator was
brought in.

At exactly 6.30 the two gun-
men gave themselves up.
They were followed out by
Mrs Guinness.

Triumph of kidnap Jenny

A   Vocabulary and Comprehension

1   After reading the article right through, answer the following general question. Choose the best answer.

This article is about

a   the brutality of some kidnappers.
b   the bravery of a woman.
c   the cleverness of the police.

2   Now answer the following, more detailed, points.

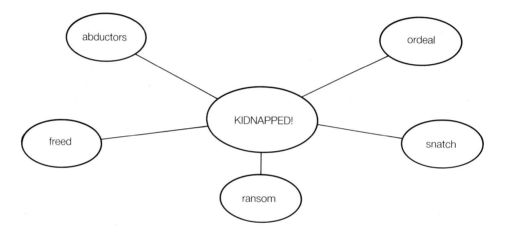

a   The above words are all connected with the theme of kidnapping. Find them in the text and then try and guess their meaning from the context. Finally, check the words in your (English–English) dictionary.
b   Explain why Mrs Guinness pretended to be angry with her husband.
c   *'John would pay more for me,'* she said *with a grin* (lines 43–5). Check the word *grin* in your dictionary. Which other words do you know connected with laughing and smiling?
d   What do you think is meant by a *softly-softly* approach (line 86)?
e   *Lair* (line 100) and *swoop* (line 102) are words normally connected with the animal kingdom. Check them in your dictionary and then explain the meanings of the words in the present context.

B   Role-play

Divide into two groups, interviewers and interviewees. Interviewers play the part of reporters sent to interview Mrs Guinness; they prepare questions, based on the information in the text. Meanwhile, the interviewees prepare to be questioned about their kidnap ordeal. After a suitable time, act out the role-play in pairs.

Triumph of kidnap Jenny

This piece appeared in the *Today* newspaper following Jennifer Guinness' release from captivity after her eight-day kidnap ordeal. Sadly, her husband has since died.

Warm-up

Ask students what they think the experience of being kidnapped would be like. How would they feel? Frightened? Lonely? Determined? How would their friends and family feel? Anxious? Helpless? Angry? How would they themselves behave or react? Would they co-operate with their captors? Make friends with them? Defy them and make things difficult for them?

A   Vocabulary and Comprehension

The answers to these questions are probably best discussed in class rather than written down. There are only a few – remember that students are going to be making up their own questions for the role-play. Similarly with vocabulary: you will have a chance to deal with any queries as you monitor students during the preparation stage.

B   Role-play

For suggestions, see General Note on page xiii.

As an alternative to an interview, imagine that Jennifer Guinness and her husband give a press conference. Two students prepare to be interviewed while the rest – journalists – prepare their questions. This format is especially suitable for a small group.

DRY DAYS ON THE LAKE

ALEXANDER FRATER
learns how to paddle a
canoe in Ontario.

ONTARIO has 62,140 miles of navigable rivers and 400,000 lakes, and provides almost unlimited opportunities for water sportsmen of every persuasion. But hereabouts it is the canoe that is king.

Just about every able-bodied Ontarian, male and 10 female alike, claims to be able to handle one. And they start young. The tiniest kids are competent to deal with cross winds or rough water, and know the wristy technique needed by the sternman to correct lateral drift and maintain a constant heading. It's called the 'J' stroke and you 20 will hear much nonsense talked about the difficulties of trying to master it. Ignore this. Even a Limey can learn the elements of canoeing in little more than an hour.

Last summer I went to try my hand at the Algonquin Provincial Park, the largest of 129 such parks in Ontario. It 30 occupies 1,776 square miles and has 580 miles of chartered canoe routes threading through scores of silent blue lakes – yet it lies only a couple of hours' drive from the high-rise glitter of downtown Toronto.

A sign at the park entrance warns that noise must be kept 40 to a minimum. A pretty, uniformed lady official told me the ruling was taken very seriously. Radios, even musical instruments, were banned.

Alcohol is prohibited, as are all food containers made of glass or tin. The rigorous bans on noise, litter and drinking are enforced by soft-voiced 50 rangers who, patrolling stealthily by canoe, can sneak up on miscreants as quietly as eels.

I reported to the centre at Canoe Lake and, before walk-

Algonquin Provincial Park, Ontario

ing down to the dock to embark, chatted to a tall, affable man named Sven who runs the centre (which provides the craft, supplies and advice) and knows more about canoes and canoeing than Hiawatha himself.

He told me it had never been so popular. In the course of a single May to October season the park registered a quarter of a million interior nights, or nights spent by holidaymakers at the various campsites – cleared areas equipped with fire pits and, in some cases, primitive outhouses.

Over coffee he warned of the dangers of fooling about with bears. I observed that this was probably the most unnecessary thing that had ever been said to me, but he insisted that people often did extraordinarily stupid things when the animals appeared – pulling faces, goading them Hemingway-fashion with a rolled-up newspaper, even trying to pose with them for pictures. *Crazy* things. You know?

The bears commonly came out at night so you never kept provisions in your tent (the bear would join you inside for an impromptu late supper) or under an upturned canoe; if it concealed supplies of chocolate cookies it could be reduced to scrap metal within minutes.

Then I went for my first Canadian canoe ride, accompanied by a youth named Sandy. I sat in the bow and he in the stern, where he briskly demonstrated a range of strokes called 'draws' and 'sweeps'.

It was a warm, sunny morning without a breath of wind. The only sounds were the splash of the paddles and the sleepy whisper of the water displaced by our passage. We slipped past small, wooded coves and little tributaries that had been turned into beaver ponds.

There were headlands planted with dense, shadowy stands of pine, spruce, balsam fir, sugar maple, yellow birch and beech. Sandy said you could make paddles from most of that stuff, but the best ones had to be cut from cherrywood.

We were heading for a couple of small adjoining lakes named Sam and Little Drummer. Forest trails connected the two. To get from one to the other you portaged your canoe, carrying it upturned on your shoulders with your head inside. If you walked into a tree it made a noise which reverberated in your ears like a giant gong.

Sam Lake, little more than a large, reed-rimmed pond, was negotiated in minutes. The sun grew hotter and my arms began to ache. The light on the water was dazzling, the water itself cold, sweet and pure enough to be scooped up and drunk fresh. By evening I could barely move for sunburn and sore muscles, but I had a terrific feeling of well-being, a huge appetite and a matching thirst, which, due to the regulations, had to be slaked with Perrier.

Dry days on the lake

A   Memory Test

After reading through the article once, test your memory (no looking back!) by doing the following multiple-choice exercises. Choose **a**, **b** or **c** in each case.

1   Ontario has
   a   40,000 lakes.
   b   62,140 lakes.
   c   400,000 lakes.

2   According to the writer, the elements of canoeing can be learnt in
   a   less than half an hour.
   b   about an hour.
   c   three or four hours.

3   The Algonquin Provincial Park is
   a   half an hour
   b   one hour
   c   two hours
   from the centre of Toronto.

4   The writer learnt that between May and October
   a   a quarter of a million people had camped in the park.
   b   it cost a quarter of a million Canadian dollars to maintain the park.
   c   a quarter of a million people had been on a camping holiday.

B   General Comprehension

Now, referring back to the text, try to answer the following questions:

1   In what way are the days on the lake *dry*? (headline)
2   What is meant by *lateral drift*? (line 17)
3   What do you think a *Limey* is? (line 23)
4   How many, literally, is a *score*? (line 33)

5   What is meant by *the high-rise glitter of downtown Toronto*? (lines 35–7)
6   What should you be careful not to do when carrying your canoe on your shoulders?

C   Vocabulary

1   What is the meaning of the following words as they are used in the article? They may be new words to you, but you should be able to have a good guess at what they mean from the context.
   a   *to sneak up on someone* (lines 51–2)
      Note: a *miscreant* is a law-breaker.
   b   *to goad* (line 84)
   c   *scrap metal* (line 97)
   d   *to head for* (line 125)
   e   *to slake* (line 151)

2   Find another word or words in the text for each of the following:
   a   very quietly, to avoid being heard (page 50, column 3)
   b   friendly (page 51, column 1)
   c   behaving in a silly way (page 51, column 1)
   d   food supplies (page 51, column 2)
   e   very bright (page 51, column 3)

D   Writing Activity

Write two signs to be put at the entrance to the park, one rather abrupt, using as few words as possible, the other more friendly and polite.

Dry days on the lake

This article contains a number of 'advanced' vocabulary items, including the names of a number of Canadian trees! However, this should not interfere with overall comprehension and general enjoyment of the piece. The exercises are straightforward and should be within the capabilities of intermediate students.

Warm-up

Ask students to discuss in pairs how many water sports they can think of in, say, three minutes. (Swimming, diving, water polo, water-skiing, surfboarding, windsurfing, rowing . . . canoeing!) Has anyone ever paddled a canoe? What is the particular attraction of canoeing?

Headline

Note that this is the subject of question 1 in section B.

Cartoon

1

2

5

6

7

4

Here is another **Peanuts** cartoon. Look closely at the pictures and the 'bubbles' and try to put the cartoon back into its correct order. There is a logical sequence!

Cartoon

See General Note on page xii.

Drugs gang held after £51 million cocaine seizure

by Neil Darbyshire, Crime Correspondent

CUSTOMS OFFICERS at Southampton found the largest haul of cocaine ever discovered in Europe – 459 lb with a street value of £51 million – then launched an international operation to trap the smuggling gang in Holland.

British, Dutch, French and German officials and police joined in 'Operation Harbinger II', which was ▇1▇ by a Customs spokesman yesterday as "a triumph of international liaison."

Eight Dutch people are in custody in Rotterdam.

10 "This is almost pure cocaine and would probably have been 'warehoused' in Holland before being ▇2▇ to other European countries, including Britain," the spokesman said.

The cocaine was ▇3▇ in the false roof of a container loaded with ceramic tiles aboard a Togo-registered ship, 20 the 7,894-ton Tagama, which called at Southampton en route from Santa Marta, Colombia to Rotterdam.

Secret search

When the freighter arrived in Southampton, cargo was ▇4▇ so that it could be re-

A Dutch official in Spijkenisse shows how the smuggled cocaine was concealed in the false roof of a goods container.

stowed. Customs officers noticed the container's padlock had been ▮▮5▮▮ , making
30 it easy to open. One officer opened the door and noticed fresh paint, which contrasted with the exterior.

The container was taken secretly to a shed where the tiles were removed. The noise produced by tapping the ceiling suggested there was a hollow space, and the internal
40 and external heights of the container differed.

The ceiling was cut away with an oxy-acetylene torch and the cocaine was found in 263 packets, each the size of a bag of sugar. It was replaced by bags of grain before the false ceiling was ▮▮6▮▮ back into place.

50 Officials, confident the crew did not know of the cocaine, allowed the Tagama to sail on.

By the time the ship reached Rotterdam, the international operation had begun. Customs men at Le Havre and Bremen were asked to watch the vessel when she visited those ports.

British Customs officers
60 joined Dutch colleagues to meet the ship at Rotterdam on Oct 2. They watched from hiding until the container was

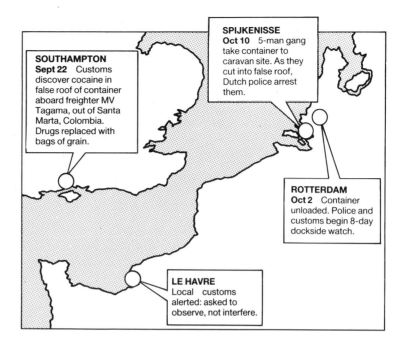

SOUTHAMPTON
Sept 22 Customs discover cocaine in false roof of container aboard freighter MV Tagama, out of Santa Marta, Colombia. Drugs replaced with bags of grain.

SPIJKENISSE
Oct 10 5-man gang take container to caravan site. As they cut into false roof, Dutch police arrest them.

ROTTERDAM
Oct 2 Container unloaded. Police and customs begin 8-day dockside watch.

LE HAVRE
Local customs alerted: asked to observe, not interfere.

▮▮7▮▮ by five people on Tuesday night.

The five took it to a caravan site a Spijkenisse and were ▮▮8▮▮ as they began to remove the false ceiling. Three
70 people were held later.

Mr Arthur Rigby, deputy head of Customs investigations, said they had netted "the Dutch marketing authorities" and a major drugs gang.

"If only 20 per cent of the cocaine had come to Britain, it would have created a new market for the drug."
80 The Customs spokesman said: "Internationally this was a bloody good job well done but the alertness of the uniformed officers at Southampton must not be ▮▮9▮▮ ."

"At any time the job could have leaked. It also depended on the container being ▮▮10▮▮ exactly as it had been before."

Drugs gang held after £51 million cocaine seizure

A   Vocabulary

1   Read the article right through first. Ignore the missing words – you should still be able to make general sense of the passage.

2   Now consider the gaps. Each one is a past participle and part of a 'passive' construction. Consider, or discuss with a partner, which words you think could fill the gaps and write them down.

3   Your teacher will now give you the ten original words from the text. (They are on the page following page 56 in the Self-Study edition if you are working alone.) Look up the meaning of any new words and see where you think each of the ten best fits.

B   Comprehension

Read the article right through again and then try to answer the following questions without looking back at the text.

1   What made the Customs officers at Southampton suspicious of the container? (Four points are mentioned altogether.)

2   What did the officers do after their suspicions had been aroused? Try to complete the sentences.
    They
    a   removed . . . .   *c*   replaced . . . .
    b   cut away . . . .   *d*   allowed . . . .

3   How were the gang eventually caught?

C   General Question

How much was the drugs haul in kilos?

D   Grammar

If only 20 per cent of the cocaine had come to Britain, it would have created a new market for the drug. This sentence, taken from the text (lines 76–9), is a 'third conditional' sentence, expressing an imaginary situation in the past. Make more sentences like this, based on the following information. Begin each one with *If . . . .*

1   The container's padlock had been tampered with and so it was easy for the Customs officers to open.

2   The Customs officers reconstructed the container very carefully and so the gang didn't become suspicious.

3   The Customs officers at Southampton were very alert and so the drugs smugglers were caught.

Drugs gang held after £51 million cocaine seizure

This is a straightforward news report, with only a few words likely to need explanation: perhaps *haul, freighter, to (re)stow, padlock, shed*.

Warm-up

Discuss the question of crime. Which crimes are regarded by society as the most serious? Provide prompts if necessary for drug-smuggling/trafficking. Turn to the headline and discuss the word *seizure*.

A   Vocabulary

Students should work in pairs and find a suitable participle for each of the gaps. There are obviously a number of possibilities for some of the gaps – you could monitor these as you go round. Encourage students to guess together the meanings of any unfamiliar words before they look them up in a dictionary. When they have all filled in a word for each gap, write the deleted words (not in order) on the board:

> *collected, unloaded, described, overlooked, welded, reconstructed, tampered with, concealed, arrested, re-exported*

Students now re-do the exercise, though some words – we hope! – will be the same. They should look up any unfamiliar words and see where they best fit.

Finally, go through the 'correct' version in class and discuss any of the words that were suggested during the first stage.

Please note that the size of each gap is not always an indication of the length of the missing word.

B   Comprehension

The questions, apart from number 3, are quite easy if the text is referred to. Better to discuss the questions together in class and see how much they can remember. This also means that students will try to express themselves in their own words, or in language they have absorbed from the text.

Pat takes good care of them

British Airways stewardess Pat Kerr does more than fly the flag. Between journeys she raises the standards for a group of Bangladeshi orphans, as Nicki Household explains

'I'M A BIT frightened of all this publicity,' says Pat Kerr. 'I feel I should go around with a label on my forehead saying, "I'm a good story."'

On first acquaintance, she might seem typical of the top-notch British Airways stewardess that she is – well-
10 groomed, friendly and charming, with beautiful waist-length blonde hair, which she wears up for work. She's got a nice flat, with its own little garden, in a fashionable part of west London that's handy for Heathrow. Whenever she has the time she pops down to visit her parents in Cornwall.

20 But she doesn't have the time very often, because the 'good story' is that she virtually leads a double life. For the last five years, she has spent almost all her free time helping to run an orphanage in Dhaka, Bangladesh. Even when she's not actually over there, she's busy working,
30 planning and raising money for 'her' children.

There are 450 of them, living in very crowded, basic, poverty-stricken conditions, which are, nevertheless, immeasurably better than those they would have suffered if the orphanage hadn't taken them in. A quarter of Bangladeshi
40 children die before their fifth birthday. Founded by the Canadian charity Families for Children, the home's policy is never to turn a child away.

Pat's involvement began when she was on a routine 'slip' (airline jargon for a stop-over) in Dhaka, and felt there must be something better to
50 do than sit around a luxury hotel feeling bored. She made

enquiries about local charity work (before joining BA she'd worked with disabled children, drug addicts and as an occupational therapist), paid a visit to the home and realised at once that 'here was something I'd always wanted to do'.
60 Soon afterwards, she took

six months' unpaid leave to go and live with the children. She had already written an article in the British Airways crew magazine about the desperate need for nappies, vitamin drops, lice shampoo and coloured pens, after which every TriStar jet that landed in Dha-

70 ka brought fresh supplies. Many crew members became almost as involved as Pat, regarding regular visits to the orphanage as part of the Dhaka run. The children know dozens of them by name; Pat Kerr, or Pat Mummy as she's called, has become far more than a friend.

80 She points out that the orphanage children put 'Mummy' after every woman helper's name, not just hers, and she praises the other people who give time and support to the project – especially BA's cabin-crew manager, Gerry Devereux, fellow stewardesses Maura McDonagh and Air-
90 drie Terenghi and BA's Director of Operations, Howard Phelps.

Pat herself is very wary of being fêted for her work. 'People want you to be a saint,' she says, 'but really I've just got an extra ration of determination and bloody-mindedness.' She likes things to be seen for what
100 they really are, and is quite worried that the two television documentaries of **The Visit**, this week and next, portray her as too self-sacrificing. 'I go there because I want to and I get a lot out of it,' she insists. 'But I love to just enjoy myself,

too. Tomorrow I'm on the Trinidad run and when I get there I
110 shall just lie in the sun.'

Pat is still a full-time stewardess, working the same hours as everyone else, but she's been allowed to fly to Dhaka more often than she would otherwise have done. British Airways have supported her to the hilt, pledging one pound for every three pounds raised
120 towards rebuilding the orphanage on a new site. Last autumn they gave Pat time off to do a Bengali language course, so she could negotiate better with local officials. She stresses that she has also received tremendous support from the Bangladeshi community in Britain.

130 She's become rather more health-and-fitness conscious since contracting amoebic dysentery and some other, less serious, tropical ailments, but completely dismisses any idea that she's endangering or sacrificing her life for the orphanage. She comments, 'Sometimes people are almost
140 determined to make out that if I hadn't got involved with the orphanage, I'd be happily married with two children in the suburbs by now [she's 34], and that that would somehow

be better! I don't agree and I don't think the two things are in the least connected. I live life as fully as I can and any-
150 thing could happen in the future, although I don't think I would ever leave the children because there's a personal bond, and I provide continuity.'

There are moving scenes in the films, especially when she rocks a tiny, wizened, skeletal baby in her arms and com-
160 ments, quietly, 'It's a rotten life for some people.' But even that, she says, has another side. 'Don't imagine I never scream at the children. There are huge rows and if a child is a bully, I say so. I got so cross with some of the older girls last time that I refused to speak to them. So they wrote to my
170 mother, whom they know, saying: "Dear Nanny, how are you, we are fine. Allah be with you. Pat Mummy come to Bangladesh, but two days she not talking to us!"'

As a stewardess, the one thing she finds difficult is being polite to rude young passengers. 'It's mostly because I'm
180 used to disciplining children at the orphanage – but also you can't help contrasting the children's circumstances.' ■

Pat takes good care of them

A Vocabulary

Read the article about the TV programme *The Visit* right through and then try to do the following language exercises.

1 What is the meaning of the following words and phrases as they are used in the text?

    a *well-groomed* (lines 9–10)
    b *virtually* (line 22)
    c *fêted* (line 94)
    d *to pledge* (line 118)
    e *to make out* (line 140)
    f *a bond* (line 154)

2 Find a word or phrase in the text with a meaning similar to each of the following:

    a of the first rank (page 57, column 1)
    b convenient (page 57, column 1)
    c extremely poor (page 57, column 1)
    d cautious (page 58, column 1)
    e giving things up for others (page 58, column 1)
    f arguments (page 58, column 3)

3 What do you understand by the word *bully*? (line 166)

B Structure

Pat Mummy come to Bangladesh, but two days she not talking to us!
It's perfectly clear what the children mean by this sentence in their letter to Pat's mother, but can you put it in more correct English? (You needn't change the delightful *Pat Mummy*!)

C Role-play

Imagine you are a newspaper reporter and that you have the opportunity to interview Pat Kerr. Prepare questions to ask her based on the information contained in the article. Another student can play the part of Pat. The reporter may read his or her questions, but the person who plays Pat should be as spontaneous as possible and try **not** to refer to the article. (Better to invent if you can't remember!)

Pat takes good care of them

This is a human-interest story, with plenty of concrete detail. It's written in a very easy prose style, with a number of passages in direct speech. There are not too many unusual words: the most useful are highlighted in the vocabulary exercises.

This kind of article lends itself very well to a role-play activity, and this is the core of the unit. There are no comprehension questions as such – the students make their own, when preparing the role-play.

Warm-up

Ask students if any of them would like to be air stewards or stewardesses. What do they think the life is like? Do they like the idea of going on 'long-haul' flights and stopping over for two or three nights in exotic places on the other side of the world? How would they spend their time? What kind of things might there be to do?

Before students begin the article, check that they know what an *orphan* is. They should then be able to deduce the word *orphanage* (check pronunciation, too – /'ɔːfənɪdʒ/).

C Role-play

See General Note on page xiii. Don't forget to encourage the 'reporters' to listen to the answers and ask follow-up questions, rather than just read out the next question! Here are just some of the possible questions:

Where do you live? Do you like living there? I know that your parents live in Cornwall – were you brought up there? (This answer can be made up – maybe yes, maybe no; perhaps her parents have retired there.) What do you do? How did you first come to get involved with the orphanage in Bangladesh? Had you had any previous experience of working with deprived people? What was the reaction of your colleagues when they heard about your work at the orphanage? Does British Airways support you in your work? (Unpaid leave, more flights to Dhaka, promise of financial aid, time off for Bengali language course.) What about the health risk of working in such conditions and surroundings? Aren't you worried about endangering your health? Do you ever get cross with the children? etc.

This role-play can also be done in the style of a 'press conference', with several reporters asking the questions. Pat could have a colleague with her to give moral support and answer some of the more general questions.

A case for smokeless zones

ALAN ROAD reports on the new moves to ban smoking in Britain's offices.

When tobacco clouds from the pipe of a pensive draughtsman activated the smoke detection system in an office of a giant multi-national company recently, fire appliances were dispatched from three neighbouring authorities to deal with the imagined danger.

There are those who would argue that in the interests of public health such sensitive detectors might be linked instead to the laboratories of local hospitals, where the far from imaginary perils of nicotine could be monitored.

While medical research has conclusively identified tobacco as a threat to the smoker's own health, the dangers to innocent bystanders of what might be called nicotine fall-out have yet to be proved beyond doubt. This has not prevented unilateralists calling for the banning of smoking in an increasing number of offices.

Nicotine traps

David Simpson, a director of ASH, the anti-tobacco group, says that unsolicited inquiries from the public about workplace policies on smoking are growing apace. 'In the past six months a lot more calls have been coming from the employers' side,' he pointed out.

Indeed, so impressed have he and his colleagues been by this phenomenon that they are planning to set up a management consultancy to advise large companies on formulating no-smoking policies.

Staff in the Normalair Garrett product support division at Bournemouth Airport were happy enough to welcome the introduction of a no-smoking rule for their newly-opened office accommodation, says personnel manager Andy Braley.

The company manufactures air conditioning systems for aircraft and employees see at first hand the nicotine trapped in valves coming back for service. 'It looks like solid blocks of treacle,' said Mr Braley, who implemented the new regime.

All too many employers seem more concerned with the wellbeing of the hi-tech equipment than of their staff. Some, says David Simpson, ignore doctors' pleas that certain workers should not be obliged to share offices with smokers. 'Yet down the corridor they have installed a mainframe computer and readily enforce a smoking ban there.'

Nor are trade unions above criticism. One has threatened legal action against a secretary who collated photographic evidence of the nuisance and danger caused by smokers in her office.

Local authorities have led the way with the introduction of office smoking bans. Ashford Borough Council are in the middle of a two-year transition period. 'It may sound long-winded,' says personnel officer John Styles, 'but the only way a decision can be enforced is if it is backed up with a collective agreement.' And so a detailed questionnaire was circulated to the council's 500 office workers, who opted – with very few exceptions – for a smoking ban.

Lawyer Gillion Howard approves of Ashford's softly-softly approach. 'You can't unilaterally slap on a no-smoking rule overnight,' she

R-R-R-R-RING

told me. A tribunal recently 110 ruled that a firm of Birmingham insurance brokers who had done just that were in breach of contract, said Ms Howard, who specialises in occupational health matters and has advised a number of Industrial Society clients on smoking policies.

Pipe dream

'If you're going to have a 120 rule that a whole building goes non-smoking, then you've got to allow employees to go into the open air and have a drag,' she warned.

While she conceded that the dangers of passive smok-ing are yet to be recognised by the courts, she forecast that the day will come when 130 evidence will be so certain and so well-publicised in the Press that employers will be obliged to take precautionary measures to protect their non-smokers. Meanwhile, she urges employers not to postpone action till then. 'Are you going to wait until you have another asbestos crisis?' she 140 asks.

One positive step they can take immediately is to recruit only non-smokers. The Royal College of Nursing who recently advertised the post of PA to the general secretary, stipulated that applications from smokers would not be welcome, she recalled.

150 'It's lawful to refuse to employ someone because they smoke,' Miss Howard emphasised. 'There is no anti-discrimination legislation for smokers.' Contracts for new recruits could, therefore, contain an undertaking that they agree to abide by no-smoking rules. 'If employees break the 160 terms of that contract, they can be counselled, warned verbally and in writing and then dismissed.'

Clean air for non-smokers may soon no longer be a pipe dream.

A case for smokeless zones

A Comprehension

Read the article right through and then try to answer the following questions.

1 What was wrong with the smoke detection system mentioned in the first paragraph?
2 What, in your own words, has *yet to be proved beyond doubt*?
3 Why did the employees of Normalair Garrett welcome the introduction of a no-smoking rule in their new office?
4 Why is it normally not a good idea to introduce a no-smoking ban without warning? (two reasons)
5 *'Are you going to wait until you have another asbestos crisis?* she asks' (lines 137–40). What do you think Gillion Howard means by this?
6 What advantage is it to an employer to recruit non-smokers?

B Vocabulary

In the context of the passage what do you understand by

1 *a fire appliance* (lines 6–7)
2 *nicotine fallout* (lines 24–5)
3 *a softly-softly approach* (lines 105–6)

4 *breach of contract* (line 113)
5 *a drag* (line 124)
6 *a pipe dream* (lines 165–6)

C Discussion

Now, in small groups, consider some or all of the following questions. First of all, here are some words and phrases which you might find useful. Discuss them with your teacher if you're in doubt about their meaning.

to ban, to impose a ban (on)	to be a nuisance
a health risk or hazard	company policy
to annoy	to enforce a rule or decision
to irritate	the rights or freedom of the individual
to harm, be harmful	personal liberty

1 In view of the findings of recent medical research, how far do you think smoking should be either banned or controlled in public places? Consider each of the following:

a the work place (office, factory, staffroom, etc.)
b cinemas, theatres, concert halls
c pubs, bars and restaurants
d nightclubs
e hospitals

f buses, trains and aeroplanes
g outdoor sports events
h indoor sports events
i parks and gardens
j the street

2 Are there any other problems brought about by smoking, apart from the health risk?

3 If you had absolute power, what laws would you introduce to control smoking? (If it is really such a

dangerous activity, should it be regarded as a drug and banned altogether?) Remember to think of the wider consequences of any proposals you make.

4   Does the smoker have rights as well as the non-smoker? If so, what can be done when these rights come into conflict?

5   Do you think that the anti-smoking lobby has become too fanatical and intolerant? After all, many smokers live to a good age, so smoking can't be that harmful, can it?

6   The smoker may say, 'It's my life, and as long as I don't annoy other people I don't see why I shouldn't smoke as many cigarettes as I like.' Is that the end of the argument, or would you have anything to say to such a person?

7   How far do you think the advertising and promotion of cigarettes should be controlled?

8   In Britain, a number of tobacco companies sponsor sporting events. Do you see a contradiction in this (smoking is not usually recommended as part of an athlete's training) or should sporting organisations just be grateful for the money, wherever it comes from?

A case for smokeless zones

This is a fairly serious article about the dangers of 'passive' smoking. It can be used as a starting point for a discussion on the whole issue of smoking – active or passive – and health.

Note on the text
ASH = Action on Smoking and Health.

Warm-up

One could introduce the topic by asking (with older students) who smokes and who doesn't, and their reasons. With younger pupils one could ask about their attitudes to smoking, and whether they intend to smoke later on in life.

Find out if everyone agrees that smoking can be harmful to health (point out that, in the UK, by law every packet of cigarettes has to carry a government health warning; is this so in other countries?). Discuss in what ways smoking can damage health – breathlessness, bronchitis, heart disease, lung cancer, etc.

Establish the concept of 'passive smoking' – the subject of the article. Ask students if they think their health is in danger from breathing in other people's smoke, or from living or working in a smoky atmosphere.

(Be careful at this stage not to pre-empt the discussion activity that follows the reading, if you intend to do it!)

The first three paragraphs of the article are rather dense and may put off a less confident reader. One can start, without any loss of context, at 'Nicotine traps' (line 31), and perhaps come back and decipher the opening paragraphs later. (In this case, begin the comprehension questions at number 3.) Students who are always complaining that things are too easy can start at the beginning!

Headline

A play on 'smokeless zones'. Normally this phrase refers to an area where the emission of smoke from chimneys is forbidden by law.

C   Discussion

Discuss the meanings of the key expressions at the beginning of the exercise. Make sure that students know how to pronounce any new words (be careful with *nuisance* and *individual*) and encourage them to introduce these words – and any others you think will be useful – into the discussion. (*Should* and *should not* will obviously be essential structures.)

Then, depending on circumstances and available space, the class could divide into groups. Appoint a chairperson for each group to control the discussion and to make sure that participants keep strictly to the particular aspect of the subject being discussed. (This usually needs close monitoring by the teacher.) Rotate the Chair to give everyone a chance of taking charge, and make sure they know their duty to encourage quiet students to speak and to tame (politely!) the over-dominant ones.

The Chair could be changed for each item in number 1. It is a good idea to use just one book, passed from one chairperson to the next.

Note: Remember to mix smokers and non-smokers, if appropriate, in each group and allow plenty of time for the discussion (30 minutes +).

For other discussion topics involving the rights of the individual, see Unit 30.

Matching Titles: Radio Programmes

These BBC radio programme 'blurbs' have become separated from their titles. By reading the information carefully you should be able to match up each programme with its correct title.

1
This Week's Composer

News, views and information for people with a visual handicap Presented by **Peter White**
Producer THENA HESHEL

2
The Natural History Programme

Digby Fairweather presents music from tonight's guests, the Cy Laurie Blue Hot Quintet.
Producer John Langridge

3
A Woman's Touch

Guest presenter, botanist David Mitchell, goes in search of golden eagles in Scotland, returns to the fossils that inspired him as a child near Moffat, and tells how to attract wildlife to inner city gardens.
Producer Grant Sonnex

4
Costing the Earth

BBC Radio Orchestra led by MICHAEL TOMALIN conducted by **Barry Wordsworth** Guest singers **Dinah Harris** and **John Brecknock** Presented by **Richard Clegg**
Producer TIM MCDONALD

5
Does He Take Sugar?

Richard Sanders asks why this country is spending billions of pounds taking nitrates out of the drinking water, when those extracted are then turned into fertiliser and sold back to farmers.
Producer Jeffrey Olstead

6
A Good Read

Michael Haydn
Minuet and Trio
(Concertino in D)
DALE CLEVENGER (horn)
FRANZ LISZT CO/JANOS ROLLA
Violin concerto in B flat
FRANZ LISZT CO/THOMAS ZEHETMAIR
(violin)
Symphony in D (P 11)
FRANZ LISZT CO/JANOS ROLLA

7
In Touch

Clara Haskil plays piano music by **Schumann, Mozart** and **Scarlatti**.
(Next week, Katia and Marielle Labeque)

8
Songs from the Shows

Brian Gear invites **Michael Marshall**, MP and **Peter Tinniswood** to pick some paperbacks.
Producer PAMELA HOWE, *BBC Bristol*

9
Jazz Parade

A magazine of special interest to disabled listeners and their families, with countrywide news and views on all matters of concern to them.
Presented by **Kati Whitaker**
Producer MARLENE PEASE

Matching Titles: Radio Programmes

See General Note on page xii.

Notes on the titles

Does He Take Sugar?   This question, asking someone else whether a disabled person takes sugar (in tea or coffee, for example) rather than asking the person concerned directly, encapsulates the insensitivity sometimes shown towards disabled people. Here, of course, it is used ironically as the title to this weekly programme for disabled listeners.

Costing the Earth   A punning title! The basic meaning here refers to environmental costs (and waste), but *to cost the earth* is also an idiomatic expression meaning 'to cost a great deal of money' – for example, *The wedding reception cost the earth.*

In Touch and **A Woman's Touch** are also titles that use puns to catch the attention.

Warm-up

Do students listen to the radio in their country? How many stations or networks are there? Are they state-run? If so, how are they financed? What kind of programmes are put on and what do they like to listen to? How many commercial stations are there?

   What do they know about British radio? How many BBC national networks are there? Do they know the differences between Radios 1, 2, 3, 4 and 5?* How is BBC radio funded? (Through the money obtained from television licence fees – see Unit 13; a separate radio licence was abolished some years ago.) Ask students if they ever listen to the BBC World Service. If in the UK, which commercial radio stations do they know?

*   **Radio 1:** mainly pop music, plus news and chat; **Radio 2:** easy listening music, including jazz, as well as comedy, drama and quiz programmes; **Radio 3:** mainly classical music, plus drama and discussion programmes; **Radio 4:** news and current affairs, plus a wide variety of speech programmes: plays, discussions, talks, interviews, readings, panel games and much more! **Radio 5:** a relatively new network featuring educational programmes for schools as well as sports commentaries and some music.

Wheels of fortune

 NO ONE COULD accuse Susi Madron of being a quitter. After her first year in business she was £14,000 in the red; and when she applied to do a small-business course at the local business school, the experts
10 turned her down because they said her idea hadn't a hope.

Five years later she's glad she didn't listen to the Jeremiahs. Last year's winner of the BBC's **Enterprise** Award, and now one of the judges for this year's event, she's proved that her gut instincts for business were right. This year the
20 turnover of her Cycling for Softies holiday company is heading for a million pounds.

The idea of pedalling your way lazily round the quiet country lanes of rural France seems such a winner that it's a wonder the big holiday tour operators didn't cotton on to it before. Picnic lunches, wayside
30 cafés, beautiful scenery and some gentle exercise to help you appreciate your dinner and hotel bed every night. It all spells a recipe for pure contentment. But it took a real family like the Madrons to recognise their own holiday had sound business potential.

Susi's commitment to test-
40 ing the hotels herself and her meticulous attention to detail have produced a highly successful package. What she offers clients is total freedom to choose their own routes and sightseeing coupled with the security of a nightly booking in out-of-the-way hotels.

 Susi, who
50 started the business in a spare room of her Manchester house, admits she's had more than a little help from her husband, Roy, a research fellow at the Manchester Business School. But even Roy's expertise didn't prevent them mak-

ing some costly mistakes in the
60 early years. The main cause of their financial disasters was the wrong kind of investment in publicity and marketing. But now they say: 'There was no way of getting that experience without buying it. We learned the hard way.'

However, their £10,000 cash prize in the BBC competition
70 last year has proved a valuable step up the business ladder. Not only did it bring freedom and favourable publicity, it also enabled them to invest in a computer.

In the days before the computer, working out individual holidays was a time-consuming process. Nearly
80 2,000 bookings last year took Susi and a colleague three months working manually to complete all the reservations.

 'This year I can run the whole thing off myself in three days,' she says happily. 'All we have to do now is put

in an invoice with the dates,
90 place and type of holiday, and the computer does the rest. It will book hotels, flights and ferries. It will tell me what we should be charging. It has released me from a lot of office work and left me a bit more time to think about where the business is going.'

With a staff of four in Eng-
100 land, 13 in France, plus a newly-acquired city-centre office in Manchester, Susi feels she is now in the league of the professionals. 'This year we're expecting an increase in business of at least 50 per cent and with this kind of growth pattern we'll soon have to add another 40 hotels.' But there is no doubt
110 about where they will be.

'Most of our customers are not cycling enthusiasts. They come because they love France, good food, getting back to nature. At the same time it's culturally very fulfilling. So we'd never dream of starting up anywhere else.' ■

Wheels of fortune

A   Comprehension

Read the article right through and then try to answer the following questions.

1   How did Susi Madron first get the idea for her business venture?
2   In what way would *gentle exercise* help you to appreciate your dinner and hotel bed? (lines 31–3)
3   What does she mean when she talks about *buying experience*? (lines 64–6)
4   What did Susi and her husband do with the £10,000 BBC prize?
5   In what way has installing a computer benefited Susi Madron?
6   What are some of the attractions of France mentioned in the text?

B   Vocabulary

1   What do you understand by the following terms as used in the text?

   a   *a quitter* (line 4)
   b   *in the red* (line 6)
   c   *to turn (someone) down* (lines 9–10)
   d   *gut instincts* (line 18)
   e   *a softy* (lines 20–1)
   f   *it's a wonder* (lines 26–7)
   g   *to cotton on to something* (line 28)
   h   *a package* (line 43)

2   Find a single word in the text for each of the following:

   a   the total value of goods or services produced
   b   happiness
   c   future possibilities
   d   personal dedication
   e   taking great care over detail
   f   professional knowledge
   g   expensive
   h   taking up a lot of time

C   Role-play

Imagine that you are a reporter. Your newspaper has sent you to Manchester to interview Susi Madron in order to write an article about 'Cycling for Softies'. Prepare some questions beforehand and carry out the interviews in pairs.

D   Writing Activity

Imagine that a customer has just walked into Susi Madron's office in Manchester. He/she has seen an advertisement for 'Cycling for Softies' and would like to know more about it. Write the dialogue that takes place between the customer and Susi Madron.

Wheels of fortune

An account of a successful business idea which won a BBC Enterprise Award: organising cycling holidays in France.

Warm-up

One might introduce this piece by discussing the pleasures of cycling. Has anyone ever been on a cycling holiday? Is it very hard work? Does it have to be? What are the advantages of a cycling holiday over, say, walking, or a motoring holiday?

Headline

A play on words, *fortune* changing its meaning here from *chance* to *wealth*.

C   Role-play

See General Note on page xiii.

Typical questions: What first gave you the idea for 'Cycling for Softies'? How did you feel when you lost £14,000 in your first year? Did you feel like giving up? How do you choose the hotels? Were you surprised to win the BBC Enterprise Award? What did you do with the money? How has the computer helped you? etc.

D   Writing Activity

Obviously the details, such as cost, exact place, airports, flight times etc. will have to be invented – unless you send for a brochure! This could serve as a simple letter-writing exercise a week or so before doing 'Wheels of Fortune'.

After having their dialogues checked, students could practise them in pairs.

Red Arrows jet crashes into row of houses

By Mark Rosselli

A JET belonging to the RAF aerobatics team, the Red Arrows, crashed on to houses in a Lincolnshire village yesterday after hitting a second Red Arrows aircraft.

The houses, two of which were badly damaged, were not occupied at the time, and both pilots parachuted to safety. More than 200 children were playing at a primary school about 250 yards from the crash. The accident happened at lunchtime as a formation of six Red Arrows was practising near the team's home base at RAF Scampton, north of Lincoln. The exact details of the incident will be established by an RAF board of inquiry, but it appears that as the formation was travelling at about 1,500 ft, the flight leader's Hawk jet was hit by a second jet.

As both spun out of control, the pilots ejected; one jet landed in a field close to the village of Welton, about three miles from the airfield. The other crashed into a row of council houses at the edge of the village, clipping two with its wing tip before crashing into a third.

Last night, the pilots were said to be in a satisfactory condition at Lincoln County Hospital, one with a broken leg and the other with minor chest and back injuries. Neither was named.

Some of those living near the crash were treated for shock; angry residents said that at the time of the accident, hundreds of children were playing outside their schools. The village also has a secondary school with 800 pupils. The Rev Brian Pritchard, chairman of the school governors at St Mary's, said: "Nobody has been hurt, thank God – but if things had been just a bit the other way, a few more

The Red Arrows flying in formation

yards, it might have been a very serious accident."

The Red Arrows use the winter to bring in new members, but all are highly experienced pilots. Their Hawks, costing £3.5m each, are stan-

dard RAF jet trainers. The unit has lost 16 aircraft since it was formed in 1965, but there have been no fatalities since 1978, when two pilots died in a crash at their home base.

Red Arrows jet crashes into row of houses

A Comprehension

Read the short news report about an air crash and then answer the following general question.

   The accident reported here was quite a serious one, but there were certain features about it that were very fortunate. How many can you find?

B Grammar Writing Activity

1 Linking words

The houses, two of which were badly damaged, were not occupied at the time . . . (lines 7–9)

This sentence contains two ideas:

A The houses were not occupied at the time (main idea).
B Two of the houses were badly damaged (secondary idea).

By using the phrase *two of which*, the writer has combined the two ideas into one sentence.

   Of which (for things) and *of whom* (for people) are very useful devices in writing (they are rarely used in informal speech) and enable ideas to be linked together. They are generally combined with words such as *all, some, both, a number, a few, two, three, each, none*, etc.

Join the following pairs of sentences together, using phrases containing *of which* or *of whom*. Note the separating commas, which must always be used.

a The two pilots are now recovering in hospital. They both ejected safely.
b The residents were very angry. Some of them were treated for shock.
c New members join the Red Arrows team in winter. All of them are highly experienced pilots.
d The Red Arrows use Hawk aircraft. They each cost £3.5 million.
    (Be careful – what does 'they' refer to?)

2 The passive

Last night, the pilots were said to be in a satisfactory condition at Lincoln County Hospital . . . (lines 36–9)

This construction, using a passive form followed by an infinitive, is very common in written style, especially in news reporting. An alternative form would be *It was said that the pilots were in a satisfactory condition at Lincoln County Hospital.*

Change the following sentences from the alternative form to the form used in the text. Be careful to keep the tenses the same. The effect of using this kind of construction (either form) is to make the information second-hand – we are only reporting what other people say.

a It was said that the residents were angry.
b It is believed that one pilot has a broken leg.
c It is said that the Hawks cost £3.5 million each.

d It is known that the new members who join the Red Arrows team are highly experienced pilots.

If the reporting refers to an earlier event (as opposed to something that is, or was, true at the time of the report, as in the last exercise), then the perfect infinitive *to have done something* or *to have been doing something* must be used.

For example: *It is said that both pilots parachuted to safety.*
                   Both pilots are said to have parachuted to safety.

Do the following in the same way. Remember that the effect is to make the report less factual and more like a rumour – 'what some people say.'

e It is said that the flight leader's Hawk jet was hit by a second jet.
f It is thought that the Red Arrows were practising a difficult manoeuvre.
g It is believed that the houses were not occupied at the time of the crash.
h It is said that more than 200 children were playing nearby.

Red Arrows jet crashes into row of houses

This is a fairly straightforward report, with not too much difficult vocabulary. The Red Arrows are the most famous aerobatics team in Britain. They give demonstrations at air shows all over the country during the summer months, and also perform in other countries. They sometimes 'fly past', too, on ceremonial occasions.

Notes on the text
RAF is the Royal Air Force.
Lincolnshire is a county in the east of England (often abbreviated to *Lincs*); *Lincoln* is the county town.
A *primary school* (lines 12–13) is for children aged from 5 to 11.
Council houses (lines 32–3) are houses owned and maintained by the local government authority (town council, county council, etc.), to whom the occupiers (tenants) pay rent.
A *secondary school* (lines 49–50) is for children aged from 11 to 16 or 18.

Warm-up

Ask the class if they've ever heard of the Red Arrows. Do they know what aerobatics is? Do they have a similar formation team in their country? How dangerous an activity is it? (Maybe not too much, since the pilots are so well trained.) What can a pilot do if his plane gets out of control? (Eject.) Would students like to be Red Arrows pilots? If so, why? What are the attractions of the job?

A Comprehension

Just one general question to get students a bit deeper into the text, which should present few comprehension problems, before they tackle the Grammar section.

B Grammar Writing Activity

Both these exercises are concerned with written rather than spoken forms.

1 Linking words
Be punctilious about commas in these non-defining clauses! It would be useful to supplement this brief exercise with some practice from other sources.

2 The passive
Note the use of the passive perfect infinitive, as well as the continuous form. Again, further exercises would be valuable as follow-up.

There is also an opportunity in this unit to revise the past continuous tense – for example, What were the team doing when the accident happened? *They were practising.* What did the pilots do when the accident happened? *They ejected.* What were the schoolchildren doing? *They were playing.* What did they do? (Imagination to the fore!)

Deep in domesticity

Jeffrey Bernard

I can't for the life of me understand why some people are so hell bent on stopping others from doing what they want to do. If I choose to close up my arteries with nicotine and then open them up again with vodka that is my business and I will. But apart from ASH there is now an organisation called Action on Alcohol Abuse which is worried about the fact that 25,000 people die from drinking every year. What else should they die from? Eating? I really would like to be left alone by organisations. AAA also says that 50 per cent of domestic murders are committed by people when they are drunk. Well, of course they are. The other 50 per cent are probably committed by supporters of AAA. You don't have to be drunk to behave like a pig.

And I know about domestic murder. I lived with a girl once

who tried to murder me. She used to burn the toast, insist on following me to the races and she was very much into sighing. You know, deep heavy sighs that make you wonder just what the hell you've done. The Guilt Machine I used to call her. She once even came to the Coach and Horses and stood in the doorway looking reproachfully at me. She didn't come inside, she just stood there and dabbed an eye with a handkerchief. She had another sort of sigh as well, much shorter and harder. That was the aggressive sigh and a nasty noise it was too. Such a terrible waste of a lovely body. Whoever it is who is responsible for putting the right brains into the right bodies really screws up sometimes. She was a dancer and I've noticed that dancers tend to be a little daft. I mean it's a funny thing to do, isn't it? I don't think it's *natural*. If you were with someone and they suddenly got up on their points, flung their arms in the air and then began to tiptoe through the tulips you'd send for a doctor or throw a bucket of cold water over them, wouldn't you? But this girl used to do her barre exercises at the ironing board. 'Just iron the bloody shirt,' I'd say and she would with a tremendous sigh. Well, she had to go and she did. She got a job dancing in Beirut.

Another attempt was made on my life by a girl who would keep telling me how very wonderful her ex-boyfriend was. Such romancing. She made him sound like St George gone to work for an advertising agency. And yet there is no organisation bent on saving us from being bored to death. It so happens that neither of those two women

would have been so boring if they had taken the odd swig from the ubiquitous bottle. I sometimes wonder, now that I'm an ex, if she tells her current chap how wonderful I was. Probably not. I threw her too many wintry smiles to make her drop her gaze. It's surprising how nasty you can make a smile if you want to. I got so good at it eventually that I could look her in the eye and make her look at the floor in five seconds. So I don't think she is referring to me as Mister Wonderful at the moment.

Which reminds me. Something rather odd; I got chatting with a bloke in a pub the other day and I'd never met him before. One thing led to another and he started telling me about his girlfriend's ex-boyfriend. After a minute or two it dawned on me that he was talking about me. I sounded really awful, from smoking in bed first thing in the morning to disappearing to Newmarket for a week with all the housekeeping money. Of course I was fascinated and I led this bloke on getting more and more information about me. Apparently, apart from smoking, racing and drinking, I have an ungovernable temper, fall asleep in restaurants or eat Indian takeaways in bed, snore and wear the same polo-neck jersey for days on end. Well, it's news to me although I must admit I did once wake up one morning to find some curry in one of my shoes. Anyway I left this man none the wiser. But who needs an agent or PR with ex-girlfriends like that. All I can say to AAA is that the majority of *attempted* domestic murders are committed by people addicted to instant coffee. That is the evil we must fight.

Deep in domesticity

Notes on the text

1 *ASH* stands for Action on Smoking and Health – an organisation that actively campaigns against smoking.
2 To be *into* something means to be very fond of something or (almost) addicted to something. For example, one can be *into* jazz or *into* health foods. To be *into* sighing is, of course, a joke on the part of the writer.
3 *Tiptoe through the tulips* (lines 61–2) is the name of a popular song.

A   Vocabulary

In the following exercises, use the context to help you decide the meaning of the word or phrase given.

1 Do you think that to be *bent on* doing something (lines 3 and 81–2) means
   a to be against doing something?
   b to be determined to do something?
   c to be afraid of doing something?

2 Do you think the *Coach and Horses* (lines 38–9) is
   a the name of a company?
   b the name of a pub?
   c the name of a riding stable?

3 Do you think the word *daft* (line 55) means
   a stupid?
   b snobbish?
   c sensitive?

4 Do you think that a *swig* (line 86) means
   a a cork?
   b a sniff?
   c a mouthful?

5 Do you think that *odd* (line 86) means
   a occasional?
   b unusual?
   c unlucky?

6 Do you think that *odd* (line 104) means
   a unpleasant?
   b silly?
   c unusual?

7 Do you think that a *bloke* (line 105) means
   a a man?
   b a publican?
   c a stranger?

8 Do you think *it dawned on me* (line 111) means
   a I was afraid?
   b I realised?
   c I was embarrassed?

9 Do you think *Newmarket* (lines 115–16) is the name of
   a a race course?
   b a supermarket?
   c a seaside town?

10 Do you think that the phrase *I left this man none the wiser* (lines 132–3) means
   a I was no wiser when I left the man?
   b the man was wiser than me?
   c I didn't give the man any information?

B   Discussion

Do you agree with the writer's first sentence? What do you think about 'campaigns' to influence other people's behaviour?
Here are a few topics for discussion – they all involve the idea of one group of people trying to influence another.

1   The sale of alcohol should be more strictly controlled.
2   Medical experiments on animals should be banned.
3   'Blood sports' such as fox-hunting and deer-hunting should be abolished.
4   Violent films should not be allowed on television.
5   Private cars should be banned from city centres.

Deep in domesticity

Students usually love this piece! It's very witty, depending entirely on language to make its points, yet should not be beyond the grasp and enjoyment of an intermediate student.

Warm-up

Ask students if they know what a 'pressure group' is. Ask if they know of any either in Britain or in their own country. What sort of influence do they have? Are they a good thing, on the whole, or not?

Note: Don't take too long over this warm-up; after all, it only gets students into the first paragraph! After that, the author veers off into talking about his ex-girlfriend, only returning to the subject of campaigners at the very end.

Exercises

Just two! Open comprehension questions on an article like this are the surest way to kill it dead. Students either understand it – and enjoy it – or they don't!

Garden cities hit the heights

UTOPIAN notions of a city in the sky have been revived – in the form of a skyscraper radically different to any yet built.

Called 'Coexistence', the strange building is by the two-man architectural practice Future Systems, which is currently the only British firm of 10 designers working for NASA, the US space agency.

Coexistence is an idea for a community of tomorrow, inspired by the United Nations prediction that by the year 2000, half the world's population will be living in cities. It is a pagoda-like tower, rising as high as 2,000 ft, over three 20 times as high as London's National Westminster Tower, consisting of alternating segments of residential apartments and offices.

No apartment is more than eight floors above landscaped parkland – for the tower carries gardens up into the sky, too. So, although the tallest 30 building may never be built the architects have developed a new principle that could be produced on a smaller scale.

Future Systems partners are Jan Kaplicky in Britain and David Nixon in America. Kaplicky says that Coexistence is a solution to the problems of high-rise living worldwide.
40 In America, he points out, living high is seen as desirable and prices of apartments tend to rise the higher they go. In Britain, the opposite is true: the social and physical failure of poorly designed tower blocks with no amenities has given high-rise a bad name, particularly for families with 50 children and old people.

The Coexistence Tower could rise as high as 2,000 ft to be the tallest building in the world, housing a community of 30,000 people. But its height is irrelevant to the concept, says Kaplicky, because it consists of repeated hu-

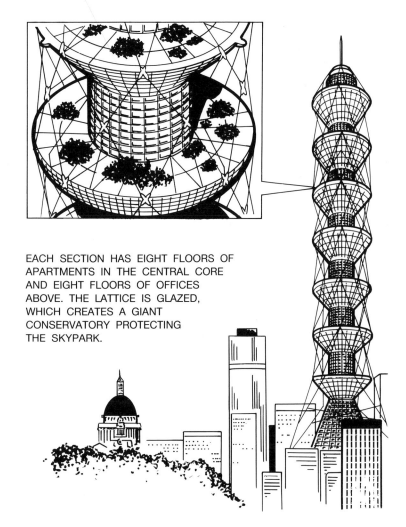

EACH SECTION HAS EIGHT FLOORS OF APARTMENTS IN THE CENTRAL CORE AND EIGHT FLOORS OF OFFICES ABOVE. THE LATTICE IS GLAZED, WHICH CREATES A GIANT CONSERVATORY PROTECTING THE SKYPARK.

man-scale modules, each 60 with a climate-controlled 'outdoors'.

'Each module has eight floors for living and eight floors for offices, with a garden beneath,' says Kaplicky. 'You could build a few modules or many. The height is not important to us.'

The construction method 70 bears out this approach. The all-steel building consists of a central cylindrical core, to be built first. As it extends upwards, inverted cone ring sections are constructed round the core and jacked upwards,

section by section, to form each layer of offices.

The flat upper surface of 80 each inverted cone then becomes a platform for a 'sky-park', which is enclosed by a glazed skin to form a giant conservatory. The skin is necessary to make the parks habitable – without it, high winds would destroy most vegetation. However, the sky-parks would be naturally 90 ventilated rather than expensively air-conditioned.

Offices are shaded from the sun by being on the underside of each cone section. Apartments in the central core, within the glazed skyparks, are protected by a moving sunshield that follows the path of the sun and doubles as a solar collector to meet energy needs.

The whole structure is externally stiffened by a tensioned steel latticework. This is a sophisticated version of the cable stays used to support television masts.

The bottom of the tower is a large upright cone containing a complete commercial quarter – hotel, shopping, leisure facilities and car parking.

The skyparks could consist of many individually-designed gardens, says Kaplicky, so removing the old tower block problem of having nowhere for the children to play.

The Coexistence project was funded by a grant from the Graham Foundation of Fine Arts in Chicago – skyscraper city. Kaplicky expects an enthusiastic response to the project in America when an exhibition of Future Systems work, just finished at London's Architectural Association, moves to Chicago shortly.

HUGH PEARMAN

Garden cities hit the heights

A Comprehension

Read the article right through and then try to answer the following five questions.

1 Why is the proposed tower to be called 'Coexistence'?
2 Why doesn't it really matter how high the skyscraper is, from the point of view of the people who will live there?
3 What is meant by a *glazed skin*? (line 83)
4 Why is such a 'glazed skin' necessary? (Check your answer to question 3 first, if you're not sure of it.)
5 What two functions will the moving sunshield have?

B Vocabulary

Find single words in the text whose meaning is similar to each of the following:

1 fundamentally (lines 1–61)
2 at present (lines 1–61)
3 forecast (lines 1–61)
4 able to be lived in (lines 62–130)
5 supports (lines 62–130)
6 financed (lines 62–130)

C Talking Points

1 What do you think are the particular problems that could arise from living in a high-rise block, and that have given them such a bad name in Britain? (lines 43–50)

2 How far do you think the planned 'Coexistence Tower' would solve these problems?

3 Would you like to work so close to where you live, even in the same building? What are the advantages and disadvantages of such a style of living?

D Speaking Activity

Explain to someone who hasn't read the article or to others in your group what the 'Coexistence Tower' is and the principal features of its design. Use your own words as far as possible, though don't be afraid to use some of the technical expressions, e.g. *cone, latticework, modules*, etc. (you will need them!). If you can, make an overhead transparency of the diagram to illustrate your talk.

Garden cities hit the heights

This piece is not as difficult as it may seem at first sight. There are a number of technical words like *cone*, *core*, *module*, *lattice*, etc., but these can be easily understood from the illustration. The prose style itself is quite straightforward – a descriptive explanation of the architectural idea, and its practical implications for everyday living.

Note: Before beginning, see **Speaking Activity** below.

Warm-up

Ask students what they think of high-rise blocks of flats. Are they regarded as desirable places to live, as in the United States, or are they generally regarded as poor-quality housing, as in Britain? What can be the advantages of living in a tower block? And what kind of problems can arise? What are the experiences of the group? See also **Talking Points** below.

Headline

A double play on words. The normal meaning of *garden city* is a (usually modern) town or urban development in pleasant rural surroundings. Here, it clearly takes on a rather different meaning. To *hit the heights* means *to reach a high level of achievement* – for example, in sport. Here the phrase is used with a more literal meaning.

C   Talking Points

1   You may have already discussed this in the warm-up. There are various points, but the chief criticisms are: poor design; low-budget building materials, resulting in rapid deterioration of the fabric; unguarded walkways, resulting in vandalism; breakdown of lifts; a feeling of isolation or imprisonment; no garden to tend and for children to play in.

D   Speaking Activity

This works very well with an overhead projector, if you have one available and can make a transparency of the diagram. With a more advanced group, the talk could serve as an introduction to the unit instead of coming at the end, as consolidation. Choose a suitable student to prepare the text at home and give a talk to the class. It can result in quite a lively question and answer session, and students are usually then stimulated to want to read the text for themselves.

Teaching scientists to see with the eyes of a journalist

' THERE they were, two men with a four-legged, round table on an uneven floor, trying to find a position where it would stand without wobbling. A familiar problem for many a householder, but could it be done, they asked. It could. The table was eventually levelled. The trick was to keep two opposite legs in contact with the floor all the time and slowly to rotate the table until all four legs stood firmly on the floor.

This was not a re-run of a 1960s Barry Bucknell do-it-yourself programme, but an Open University mathematics programme last week on the 'intermediate value theorem'. The theorem says that provided you have no steps in the floor you need never resort to pieces of folded cardboard under one leg because there is always a position of no wobble.

Here was an apparently abstract piece of mathematics being demonstrated in such an appealing way that even those who pride themselves on their dislike of maths and science could not have failed to be entertained.

So why am I telling you all this? The reason is that I have been having fun pretending to be a real journalist with this newspaper as part of a scheme to promote 'the public understanding of science'.

Nine individuals – known as media fellows – working as scientists in universities, industry or government departments are spending a few weeks with the press, radio or television to experience the way in which they handle scientific issues. The scheme was set up by the British Association for the Advancement of Science on behalf of Copus, the Committee on the Public Understanding of Science.

The media takes a lot of stick from scientists who complain about their work being distorted or misrepresented. Some of this may be justified, but the fault does not always lie with the journalist. Michael Kenward, the editor of *New Scientist* whose idea it was to launch the scheme, thinks there are far too many academics pontificating about the media who do not have a clue about how it works. 'It seemed to me', he said, 'that the best way to teach scientists about the media was to give them a chance to work alongside journalists.'

The Royal Society group which recommended the set-

ting up of Copus took a similar view. It reserved its 'most direct and urgent message' for the scientists themselves: 'Learn to communicate with the public, be willing to do so and consider it your duty to do so,' they were told. But such advice is anathema to some scientists.

Indeed, had Copus not used the title 'media *fellowships*', the credibility of the nine fellows would surely have collapsed in the eyes of scientific colleagues of such persuasion.

One of the objectives, therefore, is that the scientists should go back to their usual workplaces to encourage less enthusiastic colleagues to communicate their work more to non-scientist audiences. Scientists need to appreciate that the journalist writes to sell newspapers. Science *per se* is often only of interest to scientists. To find favour with editors, stories need also to be about the scientists working on the science and about how it relates to the reader's everyday experience.

And they should have a topical angle. Scientists may not want their work coloured in this way, but they are unlikely to see it reported otherwise in the press. They must realise, too, that stories are not written for 'peer review', but for the non-scientist. Simplifications are essential.

In the case of news stories, correspondents often have only a couple of hours to research and write stories of a specified length, which nevertheless may then be savagely cut if new stories break late in the day, or even dropped altogether. Headlines are supplied by sub-editors, so are beyond the correspondent's control.

During my brief experience with *The Independent*, I have seen a journalist's anguish over both cut prose and exaggerated headlines. But I am told that the paper could not function in any other way. On balance, the sub-editors do a good job. They were kind to me. Only one of my excursions into journalism experienced the full blast of the sub-editors' keyboard.

And what of my experience of the journalists' reporting of science? I was impressed by the strenuous efforts they make to elicit the truth. Much it seems relies on a mutual trust between correspondent and contact, built up over time. But journalism involves interpreting the facts, not simply reporting them. 'Where's the story in that?' I was repeatedly asked. It is worry over this interpretation of their work which probably concerns scientists most about talking to the press. It is a sobering thought that one single article dashed off between lunch and tea could, in theory, enhance or damage a scientific cause more effectively than any number of publications in learned journals; such is journalists' power. How wisely they use that power is, I suppose, what makes the difference between a good newspaper and a poor newspaper. **,**

Andrew Crane

Dr Crane is a research officer with the Central Electricity Generating Board

Teaching scientists to see with the eyes of a journalist

A Comprehension

Read the article right through and then try to answer the following questions:

1 What was the purpose of the demonstration of the wobbly table?
2 Why were scientists invited to work alongside journalists?
3 What kind of science articles do newspaper editors prefer?
4 Why might journalists be 'anguished' when they see their stories in print?
5 Why might they sometimes not see their stories in print at all?
6 What did the writer learn from his experience of working in a newspaper office?

B Vocabulary

1 What do you understand by the term *media fellow* (line 45)?

2 *The media takes a lot of stick* (lines 58–9). What does this mean?

3 What is the meaning of . . . *such advice is anathema to some scientists* (lines 86–8)?

4 *Per se* (line 104) is a Latin expression. What does *science per se* mean?

5 . . . *stories are not written for 'peer review'* (lines 118–19). What does this mean?

6 Can you fill in the blanks in the following sentences, all taken from the text, without referring back? A rough paraphrase is given to help you.

    a *Had Copus not used the title 'media fellowships', the cre_____ of the nine fellows would surely have col_____ in the eyes of scientific col_____ of such persuasion.*
        If Copus had not used the title 'media fellowships', some (conservative) scientists would not have been able to take the nine fellows seriously.

    b *I was im_____ by the st_____ efforts they (the journalists) make to el_____ the truth.*
        The way in which the journalists try their hardest to find out the truth made a big impression on me.

    c *It is a s_____ thought that one single article d_____ off between lunch and tea could, in theory, e_____ or damage a scientific cause more effectively than any number of publications in l_____ journals.*
        The fact that one hastily-written article could have a greater impact on a scientific cause than many serious articles in academic magazines makes one think.

C Grammar

Notice the expression *resort to* in the phrase *you need never resort to pieces of folded cardboard* (line 24). You *resort to* something when you have no alternative course of action – it is the only thing left for you to do. Note that we must use the gerund form **-ing** when referring to an action: we resort to *doing* something.

What might you have to resort to (doing) in the following situations?

1 You miss your last bus or train home.
2 You lose the keys to your house (you live alone).
3 You are travelling around on holiday and arrive at a very popular seaside town. Unfortunately you cannot find any accommodation you can afford.
4 You (and your fellow workers) cannot persuade your employer to give you a reasonable pay increase.
5 You are the Chancellor of the Exchequer (the government minister in charge of finance) and your government is in a financial crisis.

D   Pronunciation

Syllable stress

1 Put the following three-syllable words, all taken from the text, into two groups, according to their stress pattern. There is one word which does not fit either of these patterns. What is it, and what is its stress pattern?

opposite, provided, familiar, journalist, industry, entertained, department, distorted, justified, persuasion, encourage, specified, strenuous, elicit, objective

a	***b***
— · ·	· — ·

2 Now do the same with these four-syllable words. Again, there is one 'odd man out'. What is it, and what is its stress pattern?

apparently, experience, scientific, mathematics, demonstrated, communicate, anathema, recommended, appreciate, academic, correspondent, interpreting

a	***b***
· — · ·	· · — ·

E   Writing and Speaking Activities

Imagine you are one of the 'media fellows' who have just been attending the scheme outlined in the article.

Either *a*   Write a report for the Head of Department at your university on your experience with the media and what you have learnt about writing for the press;

Or *b*   Make a brief verbal presentation about what you have learnt from your experience as a 'media fellow'.

F   Experiment

Try the 'wobbly table' experiment yourself. Does the 'intermediate value theorem' work?

Teaching scientists to see with the eyes of a journalist

This looks quite a dense piece of text at first sight, but it is really very readable and a good source of media-based vocabulary for advanced students.

Warm-up

Ask students what famous scientists they know – living or historical. Ask if they know any television science programmes/presenters. Are there any 'popular' science programmes? (In the UK 'The Sky at Night', 'Tomorrow's World' and 'Horizon' are good examples.) What is the secret of their appeal? What makes a scientist into a good journalist or 'media person'?

Wizard Wilsons lift Blues

TONY PAWSON

Chelsea .... ?
Nottingham Forest .... ?

CHELSEA, who were totally outplayed in the first half, came storming back to overwhelm Nottingham Forest. Theirs was a remarkable revival in a game of flowing attacks and fluctuating fortunes.

Aiming to repeat their six-goal strike last season at Stamford Bridge, Forest were up to schedule at half-time having already put three past Niedzwiecki.

Both teams had been in impressive form in previous matches, but it was Forest who made all the early running. Pearce came driving up to initiate a series of raids down the left and each time the ball was swung across high, the Chelsea defenders looked sadly vulnerable. That flaw proved fatal when Pearce's free kick drifted over for the unchallenged Foster to dive forward and head neatly in.

The search for a scapegoat centred on Dixon, who was censored by Wicks for failing to come back and mark. That at least underlined the early pattern of play, with Chelsea more concerned to shore up their harassed defence than attempt aggression themselves.

When they did push forward it was only the prelude to further misfortune. In a quick riposte the red shirts poured forward for Webb to strand the outnumbered defenders with a clinically accurate pass which left Clough free to stroll in on goal and slide the ball home.

That stung Chelsea into instant response, Durie forcing his way past two tacklers to beat Segers with a fierce shot from an acute angle. For a brief period Chelsea maintained their insistent pressure and only a fine save by Segers denied Wood, but soon after they were again caught flat-footed as Forest broke fast. Clough ran free down the left and when he crossed, there was Wilkinson to dive forward and bounce his header in off the far post.

There was a second-half transformation as the busy Kevin Wilson was brought on to replace the lackadaisical Dixon. His influence helped to give the Chelsea team greater purpose, and the pressure now was on Forest.

For the second successive match Brian Clough had to watch his team surrender a 3–1 lead. A patient build-up between Hazard and Clive Wil-

son soon made the opening for Durie once more to apply a forceful finish. Clive Wilson then ran free to equalise with a low shot past Segers.

There was no slackening in the hectic pace as Niedzwiecki saved at full stretch from Glover, and Chelsea's Clarke then came storming forward to

beat Segers with a shot that was cruelly deflected past the goalkeeper.

RESULTS TABLE
BARCLAYS LEAGUE – Division 1

Charlton	(0)	0	QPR	(1)	1	
			Coney	7,726		
Chelsea			Nottm For			
Coventry	(0)	0	Man U	(0)	0	
				27,125		
Derby	(0)	0	Portsmouth	(0)	0	
				15,071		
Everton	(0)	0	Tottenham	(0)	0	
				32,389		
Newcastle	(0)	1	Wimbledon	(2)	2	
McDonald (pen)			M. Thomas (og),			
			Cork	22,684		
Oxford	(1)	2	Luton	(2)	5	
Slatter, Foyle			B. Stein, Breacker,			
			Nwajiobi, Hill,			
			Harford	6,804		
Southamptn	(0)	1	Sheff W	(1)	1	
Clarke			Chapman	12,526		
Watford	(0)	0	Norwich	(0)	1	
			Bruce	11,724		
West Ham	(0)	1	Liverpool	(0)	1	
Cottee			Aldridge (pen) 29,865			

LEAGUE TABLE

	P	W	D	L	F	A	Points
QPR	6	5	1	0	9	1	16
Man Utd	6	3	3	0	10	4	12
Chelsea	6	4	0	2	13	8	12
Tottenham	6	3	2	1	9	4	11
Wimbledon	6	3	2	1	9	5	11
Nottm For	6	3	2	1	10	8	11
Coventry	6	3	1	2	8	8	10
Everton	6	2	3	1	6	2	9
Liverpool	3	2	1	0	7	3	7
Southmptn	6	1	4	1	9	9	7
Norwich	6	2	1	3	5	6	7
Arsenal	5	1	2	2	8	5	5
Derby Cnty	4	1	2	1	2	2	5
Luton	6	1	2	3	8	10	5
West Ham	5	1	2	2	6	8	5
Oxford	5	1	2	2	8	12	5
Portsmth	6	1	2	3	6	16	5
Newcastle	5	1	1	3	4	7	4
Watford	5	1	1	3	2	5	4
Sheff Wed	6	0	2	4	3	12	2
Charlton	4	0	0	4	3	10	0

Wizard Wilsons lift Blues

A   Comprehension and Deduction

Read the report of the first division league match between Chelsea and Nottingham Forest and then try to answer the following questions. You may like to do this exercise in pairs.

1 What is the name of Chelsea's ground?
2 What is the name of Nottingham Forest's manager?
3 Which team wears red shirts?
4 What colour does the other team wear?
5 Who is Nottingham Forest's goalkeeper?

6 Why was Dixon taken off at half-time?
7 Who scored first for Chelsea?
8 How many goals were 'headers'?
9 What was the score at half-time?
10 Who won the match and what was the final score?

B   Talking about football (and other team sports, e.g. rugby, hockey, basketball)

Do you know how to ask and answer the following questions about sport in English? See how you would manage in the following situations (imagine that the two teams referred to are the famous north London rivals, Arsenal and Tottenham Hotspur (Spurs)). The questions are not always as simple as they may seem!

1 You arrive at a friend's house, where a football match is on TV. You want to know the names of the teams.
   a What do you ask?
   b What is the answer?

2 You want to know what the situation is in the match.
   a How do you ask?
   b How do you answer for each of the following scorelines?
      i) Arsenal 0   Spurs 0
      ii) Arsenal 1   Spurs 1
      iii) Arsenal 2   Spurs 1

3 You want to know who scored Arsenal's goals. How do you ask?

4 You want to know how much of the match you have missed. How do you ask?

5 You want to know how much time is left. How do you ask?

6 Imagine that you arrive at your friend's house after the match has finished. How do you ask what happened?

7 You actually support Manchester United, but you haven't yet heard today's results. What do you ask your friends?

8 Here are some results: Oxford United 2   Luton 5
                                                 West Ham 1   Liverpool 1

Can you fill in the gaps in the following sentences?
  a Oxford were playing at _____.
  b Luton were playing _____.
  c Luton _____ (the match) five two.
  d Oxford _____.
  e Luton _____ Oxford.
  f Oxford _____ _____ Luton.
  g West Ham _____ _____ Liverpool.
  h The match was a _____.
  i The score was one _____.

C Dialogue

Talk about the results of the other matches, working in pairs. One student looks at the league table and asks questions about the various teams; the other answers by referring to the results table. Remember to use 'they' in your answers.

Example: *How did Wimbledon get on? They won, two one.*
                    How did Watford get on? They lost, one nil.
                    How did Derby get on? They drew nil nil.
                    Who scored for QPR? etc.

Wizard Wilsons lift Blues

This is quite a difficult piece and something for advanced students to get their teeth into. However, it is not necessary to understand every word in order to answer the comprehension questions, which involve picking out facts and making deductions. Question 10 in section A is difficult though, as the word 'goal' is hardly mentioned at all!

Note

1   Some players have been transferred to other clubs since this piece was written. There have been a few changes in the First Division too!
2   The top 22 English clubs now play in the Premier League (since the beginning of the 1992–3 season); the remaining 70 play in Divisions 1, 2 and 3.

Warm-up

Ask students which names of British football teams they know. Which London clubs do they know? (Arsenal, Tottenham Hotspur (Spurs), West Ham, Queens Park Rangers . . . Chelsea.) Whereabouts in London is Chelsea? Where is Nottingham? In which year did Nottingham Forest win the European Cup? (1979 and 1980!) How many divisions are there in the English league? (Four – see Note above.) And in Scotland? (Three.) When are matches usually played? (On Saturday afternoons at three o'clock. There is usually just one match on a Sunday, which is televised live.)

A   Comprehension and Deduction

Clues to the answer to question 10 (for non-footballers!):

First goal (Nottingham Forest) – *flaw proved fatal* (line 23); *head neatly in* (lines 26–7).
Second goal (Nottingham Forest) – *clinically accurate pass* (line 44); *slide the ball home* (lines 46–7).
Third goal (Chelsea) – *instant response* (lines 48–9); *beat Segers* (line 51).
Fourth goal (Nottingham Forest) – *bounce his header in* (key word) *off the far post* (lines 62–3)
Fifth goal (Chelsea) – *surrender a 3–1 lead* (lines 74–5); *Durie . . . apply a forceful finish* (lines 78–9)
Sixth goal (Chelsea) – *equalise with a low shot past Segers* (lines 80–1)
Seventh goal (Chelsea) – *beat Segers with a shot that was cruelly deflected past the goalkeeper* (lines 87–9)

B   Talking about football and other team sports

Clearly, there is more than one possible way of asking (and answering) the questions in this section, but the ones suggested in the answers are extremely common. They are not, though, very often on the lips of students, perhaps because these phrases tend to be rather condensed and idiomatic – it would be surprising if students got many of them right! (Even score-lines are usually incorrectly said by students: *two to one* is not a score but a bookmaker's odds! See questions *2b* and *8c*.) Section B, therefore, is really a way of introducing students to these idiomatic question forms (and answers). They should be learnt and practised before embarking on the dialogue in section C.

C Dialogue

A note on the results table
1 Half-time scores are shown in brackets.
2 Goal-scorers' names are given (*pen.* = penalty; *o.g.* = own goal – unfortunate!)
3 The large number on the right refers to the number of spectators at the match, or the 'size of the crowd'. Sometimes this figure is referred to as *the gate* – for example, *the highest/lowest gate of the year*.

A note on the league table
P, *W*, *D*, and *L* stand for matches *played*, *won*, *drawn* and *lost*. *F* and *A* stand for goals *for* and goals *against*. Three points are awarded for a win, one point for a draw (students can be asked to work this out – not difficult!).

A note on team names
Abbreviations are used for convenience in both the results and the league tables. The following is a guide to the pronunciation of team names.

Name of team or abbreviation	Pronunciation
QPR = Queens Park Rangers	Usually *QPR* or *The Rangers*.
Man Utd. = Manchester United	*Manchester United* – sometimes *Man United*, especially by the team's own fans!
Tottenham	/ˈtɒtnəm/ The team's full name is Tottenham Hotspurs, and so they are often called *Spurs*.
Nottm For. = Nottingham Forest	/ˈnɒtɪŋəm/ *Forest* – sometimes just called *Forest* by the people of Nottingham!
Southmptn = Southampton	/saʊˈθæmptən/
Norwich	/ˈnɒrɪtʃ/
Arsenal	/ˈɑːsnəl/
Derby Cnty = Derby County	/ˈdɑːbɪ/ *County* is usually omitted when speaking casually.
Portsmth = Portsmouth	/ˈpɔːtsməθ/
Sheff. Wed. = Sheffield Wednesday	*Sheffield Wednesday* – or just *Wednesday* by Sheffield people, to distinguish the team from Sheffield United.

The point of using the league table in the pair work activity is so that the students asking the questions are not themselves looking at the answers! The results table can be covered and they can just pick a team from the list at random.

Other possible questions

What (and where) was the biggest/smallest crowd of the day? (Not 'how many spectators . . .'.)
What was the crowd at Derby?
What was the crowd at Norwich? (Answer: they were playing away – try again!)

You could also use the league table to draw attention to questions using the present perfect tense, compared with the past tense for Saturday's results. For example, *How many matches have QPR played/won/lost/drawn this season (or so far this season)? How many goals have they scored? How many goals have they had scored against them? How many goals did they score on Saturday?*

Note: We wouldn't say 'How many points have they scored?' but *How many points have they got?*

Cartoon

One more **Peanuts** cartoon – slightly longer this time. Study the pictures and texts carefully and try to put the cartoon back into its correct sequence.

1

2

3

4

5

6

7

8

9

10

Cartoon

See General Note on page xii.

SHAPING UP NICELY

1 THE START could scarcely have been less auspicious. There we were, waiting in the aircraft on the tarmac with the prospect of a 12,000-mile journey ahead of us, when our cogitations were interrupted by the voice of the pilot over the intercom. Regrettably, he said, there would be a two-hour delay before we could be airborne.

2 All kinds of thoughts pass through the mind at such times, not least that flying to the other side of the world can be an exceedingly tedious business. Since that day I have greeted any lessening of time spent in the air as manna from heaven.

3 So it's good news that you can now fly from Australia to Britain with Cathay Pacific Airways in just 23 hours, compared with almost a week in the days of the flying boats. The next time I will be looking forward to the experience, particularly as the airline has promised that I will Arrive in Better Shape.

4 Here a word of explanation might be necessary. Mindful of the tedium of long air journeys, and their effects on passengers, Cathay Pacific, which is based in Hong Kong and is now owned by the Swire Group, is wooing customers with an in-flight service which it believes is superior to that of its competitors. The four words are the substance of the matter.

5 Formed in 1946 by two wartime pilots, the Australian Sydney de Kantzow and the American Roy Farrell, Cathay Pacific has grown into one of the largest – and most successful – airlines in the region, offering flights to Europe from Australia and New Zealand as well as points in South East Asia.

6 In some respects the Far East airlines do have the edge

TIM WARE FLEW WITH CATHAY PACIFIC

'The service was superb!'

over their European and North American counterparts. A willing smile and a desire to please are not just the fantasy of advertising copy-writers. They do exist and they have become, for many passengers, as much a part of the travel experience as the good food, free drinks, latest film and warm towel.

Below: *Cathay Pacific has a loyal following and a fine reputation for service and exceptionally good food.*

7 Cathay's in-flight service, in my experience, is caring without being ostentatious. The food would do credit to a good restaurant in Sydney or London, or anywhere else for that matter. In first class, the self-indulgence stretches from the fully-reclining sleeperette seats to caviar and freshly cooked eggs for breakfast – quite an achievement at 30,000 feet!

8 Those travelling Business or Tourist Class don't go wanting either. For Business Class passengers, there's a separate check-in desk at the airport, priority baggage handling and specially contoured seats. There's a glass of champagne before take-off, a choice of seats when you make the reservation, a choice of meals on board and even a chauffeur-driven limousine, should you need one, when you arrive at your destination.

9 For Economy Class passengers there are free drinks, free films and entertainment, and the chance to have a special light meal (to enable you to arrive in better shape, presumably) if you order it beforehand.

10 Air travellers like to be cos-

seted en route and, increasingly, they are looking to the airlines to help ease their passage on the ground, too. For all but the most dedicated airline buff, the flight is only the means to the end – the holiday or the business trip.

11 With this in mind, Cathay Pacific has drawn up its Stay a While programme of hotel packages, offering its passengers good accommodation at competitive rates.

12 In London, the list of a dozen or so hotels includes establishments like Berners, in the heart of the West End, the Kensington Palace in Kensington Gardens, which is only a few minutes walk from the Knightsbridge shopping area, and the Forum in South Kensington. Australians are not the only ones who will find rates are astonishingly low for London.

13 Just as valuable, in its own way, is the London Explorer Pass, which comes free to those Cathay Pacific passengers spending three or more nights in the capital. The pass entitles you to unlimited travel on London's buses or underground system.

14 Armed with this, visiting the places everyone wants to see when they come to London – and I suppose the Houses of Parliament, Tower of London, Buckingham Palace and Westminster Abbey are top of the list – is child's play compared with getting around the capital on your own. Better still, it'll enable your holiday budget to go that much further.

15 Certainly the airline business has come a long way since the days when it concerned itself simply with the job of providing a ticket from A to B. After-sales service has become as important as it is in the job of selling a new car. You can now look forward to being pampered like a pet lamb long after the aircraft has touched down.

Shaping up nicely

A   General Comprehension

Read the article right through and then answer the following general question. Choose the best answer.

This article is about

a   the advantages of travelling by air.
b   the advantages of flying with Cathay Pacific.
c   the needs of passengers on a long-haul flight.
d   the importance of providing 'after-flight' service to passengers.

B   Detailed Comprehension

Now discuss, with a partner or in a group, the answers to the following, more detailed, questions about the article.

1   *The four words are the substance of the matter* (paragraph 4). What four words is the author referring to?

2   What does this phrase mean exactly? (Check your answer to the previous question first, if you're not sure of it!)

3   What do you think *manna from heaven* (paragraph 2) means in this context?
    a   Something unforeseen.   **c**   Something very surprising.
    b   Something undeserved.   **d**   Something very pleasant.

4   What do you understand by *in-flight* service (paragraph 7)?

5   *Those travelling Business or Tourist Class don't go wanting* (paragraph 8) means that these passengers
    a   don't ask for extra attention.   **c**   don't want anything.
    b   are well looked after.   **d**   are difficult to please.

6   *Should you need one* (paragraph 8) means
    a   do you really need one?   **c**   if you need one.
    b   you might need one.   **d**   you should need one.

7   *Cosseted*, in paragraph 10, is very similar in meaning to which word in paragraph 15?

8   What is the main benefit of the London Explorer Pass (paragraph 13)?

9   *The airline business has come a long way* (paragraph 15). This means that the airline business has
    a   improved a lot.   **c**   flown many passengers.
    b   flown many miles.   **d**   tried to help its passengers.

10   The headline is a pun, or play on words. Can you explain it?

11   Lastly in this section, a test question.
    When an aircraft is on the 'runway' it is ready to 'take off'. What does it do before that, when it is on the *tarmac* (paragraph 1, line 4)? (Apart from 'wait'!)

C   Vocabulary

1   What is the meaning of the following words
and phrases as used in the article?
  a   auspicious (paragraph 1)
  b   cogitations (paragraph 1)
  c   to woo (paragraph 4)
  d   to have the edge over (paragraph 6)
  e   ostentatious (paragraph 7)
  f   self-indulgence (paragraph 7)

2   Find words or phrases in the text with
similar meanings to each of the following:
  a   take off (paragraph 1)
  b   boring (paragraph 2)
  c   reduction (paragraph 2)
  d   enthusiast (paragraph 10)
  e   amazingly (paragraph 12)
  f   easy to do (paragraph 14)

D   Role-play: awkward passengers

First, discuss with your teacher or think about the various ways of

1   making polite requests.
2   saying *yes* or *no* politely.
3   making complaints.
4   dealing with complaints.

Then write down, in note form, as many requests and complaints as you can think of that an air
passenger might have (be imaginative!)
     Now, working in pairs, play the parts of the 'awkward passenger' and the air steward or
stewardess. After a few exchanges, reverse the roles.

Alternatively, if space and furniture allow, convert the classroom into an aircraft cabin, with
'passengers' sitting in twos and threes. Stewards and stewardesses walk up and down and deal with
all the problems.

Shaping up nicely

There are a few difficult words and phrases in this travel piece, but not too many. Don't let students be discouraged during the first reading – for example, by the word *auspicious* in the first sentence! They should keep going, and try to get an overall grasp of the passage.

Warm-up

Have you ever flown? (Or, has anyone <u>never</u> been in an aeroplane?) What is your attitude to flying? Do you enjoy it? Do you get nervous? (before the flight? just before take-off? during take-off? before landing?) What aspects of in-flight service do you most appreciate, or don't you care, so long as you get to where you're going safely? What aspects of travelling by air do you find tedious?

Headline

This is derived from Cathay Pacific's slogan 'Arrive in Better Shape' (paragraph 3). The phrase is an idiom meaning *performing in a promising way* in the context of a new venture or activity. See section B, question 10.

Comprehension and Vocabulary

While the comprehension questions are probably best done together in class, the vocabulary exercises could well be done at home, with the aid of a dictionary, if class time is short.

D   Role-play

Discuss the language of polite requests and complaints, and how to deal with them, in an earlier lesson if possible, and use the role-play to practise/consolidate.

Give students time to write down a number of things to ask for/complain about during a flight. When ready, they can act out in pairs, as directed in the students' notes. Monitor the pairs, and have a general feedback session at the end if necessary.

Alternatively, if space and furniture allow, convert the classroom into an aircraft cabin, with 'passengers' sitting in twos and threes. Choose some students to be stewards and stewardesses (perhaps those who really have such ambitions!). Take them aside and revise with them the language they will need to deal with questions and complaints – plenty of *Of course, madam* and *Certainly, sir*, as well as *I'm terribly sorry* and *I'll . . .* (not *I'm going to . . . !*).

While you are with the flight crew the passengers can be preparing their questions. Check these for correctness, and try to ensure that not too many are duplicated. Encourage students to be imaginative – for example, *I think I'm going to have a baby*, or even manic *Stop the plane, I want to get off!*. Stewards and stewardesses then come in and walk up and down, dealing with the problems. This session can be fun, but do allow enough time, both for preparation and the activity itself.

Behind the door of 10 Downing Street

by Christopher Jones

1 Number 10 Downing Street presents an unrevealing face to the world. But that unexceptional front door opens on an extraordinary maze of corridors and winding staircases, of grand reception rooms and ordinary offices, of bustling officials and ordered calm. To an outsider it seems a hopeless tangle of activity, quite impossible to sort out, but really it is a rather cosy household, where everybody knows everybody else very well, and where a quite perceptible loyalty exists between the groups of people who work there.

2 The famous building is, in fact, two houses. The front door was on one of a number of large houses built by a deplorable 17th-century opportunist and profiteer, Sir George Downing. He built the houses in about 1680 with blood money earned from selling his former Cromwellian friends to Charles II after the Restoration: they went to Tyburn to be hanged, drawn and quartered. He did not live to see the development completed, and his speculation came to some good when his grandson used the profits to found Downing College, Cambridge.

3 Immediately behind Downing Street, in the area that for centuries was taken up by the Royal Court of Whitehall, there was a large house which eventually became the home of Baron Bothmar, the Hanoverian Ambassador. When he died, George II offered this house and the one with its entrance in Downing Street, which are now knocked together, to Sir Robert Walpole as his official residence. Walpole declined the houses as a gift – the cost of the work that had to be done to them would have been prohibitive – but he accepted them in 1735 in his capacity as First Lord of the Treasury, a post which he held

Number 10 Downing Street

until 1742. He was in effect Britain's first Prime Minister, but the position was not officially recognized and Walpole himself rejected the title.

4 The muddled origins are evident today. A very long corridor, which now leads eventually to the Cabinet Room, joins the original Downing Street house to the one at the back. At the end of the corridor the new visitor finds that having entered the building on the ground floor he is now, without going up a single step, on the first floor. Looking at the outside of Downing Street, no one would know that the houses were built on a very steep slope indeed, and the great curving staircase in the rear part of the house goes down a floor below the entrance hall.

5 A visitor to Number 10 today (assuming he first gets past the stringent security checks which cut the street off from Whitehall) meets the policeman who is always on duty outside. The constable gives one knock only on the lion's-head knocker – touched for luck by soldiers during the First World War – and the uni-

formed attendant opens it from the inside.

6 Once in the hallway, with its black-and-white-chequered marble floor and large display of flowers in the marble fireplace, visitors wait until an official comes to greet them. The atmosphere is one of calmness and lightness. A previous occupant, Mrs Thatcher, did not like dark colours, and had heavy paint and baize-covered doors removed wherever possible. Heavy baize was one of her particular dislikes, but she allowed it to remain as a protective cover on a fine table in the ante-room of the Cabinet Room where Ministers put their red official boxes before a Cabinet meeting. She never managed to get the brown baize removed from the Cabinet table itself. The table narrows at each end so that the Prime Minister, who sits in the middle of one side, can see each member. It is officially described as boat-shaped – or, less reverently, coffin-shaped.

7 The Cabinet Room itself is much brighter than it used to be. Until the extensive reconstruction of Downing Street in the 1960s, the room was surrounded by heavy mahogany bookcases. Only two of these remain at one end of the room, half-hidden behind two pillars introduced some years ago when the room was enlarged. The carpet, like most of those in the official part of Number 10, is in light gold, and the Victorian mahogany chairs are newly upholstered in tan hide.

8 Only one picture is allowed in the Cabinet Room – of Sir Robert Walpole himself, by Van Loo or his studio. There are three portraits of Sir Robert in Number 10. The other two are prints on the main staircase and in the entrance hall. Many paintings in Sir Robert Walpole's collection were sold by his grandson Horace to

Catherine the Great of Russia and are now in the Hermitage in St. Petersburg.

9 Many prime ministers – Churchill among them – used the Cabinet Room as their office. But Mrs Thatcher preferred a much smaller room which prime ministers once used as their bedroom. When she first went to Number 10 this room was, she recalls, decorated with dark green flock wallpaper. It would have taken 20 years to get it changed going through the official process, so she had it replaced at her own expense. Today, the room has pale grey striped paper and oyster satin chairs. Behind the desk – not very grand for a Prime Minister – is a painting by Zoffany of the Rosoman family, and at the far end of the room a magnificent Queen Anne walnut bureau bookcase from the Victoria & Albert Museum.

10 There is relatively little in Number 10 which links it with its historic past. There is a rather rickety, red-leather-topped desk in a drawing room, said to have belonged to William Pitt the Younger, but hardly any other reminders of its former tenants. In the entrance hall, as well as the picture of Walpole, is a portrait of Lord Chatham, but he, like many of the earlier prime ministers, did not live here. Premiers often remained in their own London homes and let other ministers – the Chancellor of the Exchequer or high government officials – take the house.

11 Former prime minister Edward Heath did some restoration to the formal part of the house during his term of office. After the long and expensive reconstruction of the 1960s, the State Apartments used for formal entertaining had been left featureless, with unimpressive paintings and furniture. Edward Heath had the walls hung with splendid patterned silk to recreate the former Blue and White Drawing Rooms, and with yellow silk in the Pillared Drawing Room, where the largest receptions are held. He also had the wood panelling of

the large dining room lightened, and hung fine English and French pictures. Lady Wilson had the splendid collection of portraits of prime ministers restored to the walls of the main staircase (Lady Dorothy Macmillan had had them put in a side passage) ranging from Walpole at the bottom to James Callaghan (the only one in colour) at the top.

12 In the small dining room there are portraits and busts of British scientists Sir Isaac Newton, Sir Humphry Davy and Edmond Halley, and among the splendid Adam furniture of the White Drawing Room, traditionally the boudoir of the prime minister's wife, there is a series of Staffordshire figures of British politicians.

13 Away from the splendour of the formal rooms, Number 10 is solidly down to earth. The famous Garden Girls, the dozen or so secretaries who deal with the many thousands of letters that a prime minister gets every week, work in the two Garden Rooms, looking out over the lawns and rose beds that extend behind Number 10 and Number 11. On the wall behind the electric typewriters and word processors is a plaque recalling wartime in these rooms, then shored up by heavy wooden supports, when Churchill and the King met to discuss the war.

14 Close by are the rooms of the Principal Private Secretary and the Private Secretaries. Their long working days are dominated by three brass ship's clocks, one showing London time, one Washington time and one the time in Moscow, or in another part of the world where there is a crisis. The Private Secretaries divide up specific areas of government – foreign affairs, economy, and so on. There is the atmosphere of an old-fashioned solicitor's office, but the staff is surprisingly young, high-fliers whose Civil Service careers take them to Number 10 for two or three years before moving on upwards.

15 The Prime Minister has a relatively small private flat in the building, carved out by the Chamberlains from the old servants' rooms at the top of the house. Surprisingly, there is no official domestic staff and just two cleaners. There is a dining room that can seat eight people and a small, long and narrow kitchen, with a well-stocked freezer but little else. "You can't sit down in here," said one occupant recently. "I've always wanted a nice big kitchen with a table that you can sit at, but we haven't got that here." Surely not too much for a Prime Minister to ask for at Number 10.

Portraits of former prime ministers line the walls of the main staircase

Behind the door of 10 Downing Street

A   Comprehension

As this article is rather a long one, read the following questions first, to give you an overview of the piece. Then, after reading the article right through, try to answer them.

1   Explain how the ground floor at the front of Number 10 becomes the first floor at the back.
2   Which house was built first, the one at the front or the one at the back?
3   What security measures are in force to protect the Prime Minister at Number 10?
4   What is the purpose of having a boat-shaped table in the Cabinet Room?
5   Who was Sir Robert Walpole?
6   Why did Mrs Thatcher pay for the redecoration of her office herself?
7   Why, at Number 10, are there so few objects to remind one of prime ministers of the past?
8   What does the visitor see on the walls as he/she goes up the main staircase?
9   What do you think a *high-flier* is? (paragraph 14)
10 What is the problem with the kitchen?

B   Vocabulary

1   What is the meaning of the following words as used in the text? Most of them are not easy to define, and are probably best discussed together in class, or with a friend.

   a   *bustling* (paragraph 1)   *d*   *rickety* (paragraph 10)
   b   *tangle* (paragraph 1)   *e*   *down to earth* (paragraph 13)
   c   *cosy* (paragraph 1)   *f*   *shored up* (paragraph 13)

2   Find words or phrases in the text which have similar meanings to each of the following:

   a   ordinary (paragraph 1)   *d*   too expensive (paragraph 3)
   b   morally shocking (paragraph 2) *e*   confused (paragraph 4)
   c   refused to accept (paragraph 3) *f*   very strict (paragraph 5)

C   Research Activities

1   How many British Prime Ministers (or their wives!) are mentioned in the article? Make a list.
2   If you're interested in British history, look up some of the names in an encyclopaedia and find out more about them.
3   Find out more about Robert Adam (paragraph 12), the great eighteenth-century architect and furniture designer.
4   Three British scientists are mentioned in paragraph 12. Do you know what they are famous for? Use an encyclopaedia to find out what they discovered or invented.
5   Do you know the name of the Prime Minister's official country residence, often used at weekends? You may have to do some research!

D   Talking Points

1   This article probably contains quite a lot of information that you didn't know before. But did any of it surprise you? Compare your reactions with those of others in your group.
2   What do you know about your own President's/Prime Minister's official residence?

Behind the door of 10 Downing Street

This article about the history of the British Prime Minister's residence is not as demanding as its length might suppose. However, students might find the beginning, which deals with the early history and construction of the house, slightly heavy going. If so, they could begin at paragraph 5 with no loss of understanding, and start the questions at number 3 in section A.

Warm-up

Introduce the lesson by asking students the name/address of their own Prime Minister's or President's residence. Do they know where the British Prime Minister lives? Have they ever seen the outside of the house? (Were they surprised? It looks very ordinary!) What do they imagine it's like inside? How long has it been in use? (About 250 years.) What <u>kind</u> of changes would successive Prime Ministers probably make? (Elicit such things as furniture, colour schemes, carpets and curtains, paintings, etc.)

A Comprehension

Note the suggestion to students to read through the questions before they begin the article.

B Vocabulary

1   Students should be able to have a good guess at the meaning of all these words from the context. Point out, if necessary, that *bustling officials* contrasts with *ordered calm*, in the same way as *grand reception rooms* and *ordinary offices* are in contrast. This exercise is best done together in class, or perhaps with students working in pairs.

Matching Titles: Films

Here are some film 'blurbs' with the wrong titles. Can you match them up correctly? If you read carefully, it's not too difficult – each blurb contains at least one clue!

1
The Journey

Director Rossellini returned to the war setting of one of his earliest triumphs for this fascinating account of three escaped allied prisoners caught in the Italian surrender.

2
One Hour to Zero

She's not a person, it's a port in Mexico, to which Gary Cooper and Burt Lancaster are escorting a countess with stacks of gold. Lively characters, imaginative use of landscapes, abrasive comedy, punchy action: everything is perfectly balanced. And Lancaster's villainous smile is devastating.

3
The Thing from Another World

John Wayne in one of his more off-beat roles as a German officer trying to sail his freighter out of Australian waters as World War Two begins. Lana Turner is also on board as an adventuress and spy. A watchable adventure, though the casting throws some of the drama askew.

4
The Sea Chase

Classic RKO thriller where menace lurks in every shadow and staircase. Sets, photography, an amazing dream sequence and Peter Lorre all contribute to the bizarre Germanic atmosphere. A most rewarding oddity.

5
Night in Rome

'An intellectual carrot – the mind boggles!' Dialogue like that certainly keeps us smiling, yet this science-fiction drama deserves its reputation for high dramatic tension and intelligence.

6
White Corridors

Politics and romance cause problems for travellers trying to leave Hungary after the 1956 uprising. Director Anatole Litvak gives the film that cold consommé feeling, though it's interesting as a Hollywood response to world events.

7
Vera Cruz

A minor triumph for British cinema, recounting a hospital's daily round with an expert blend of emotional drama, diverse characters, and comic relief. Director Pat Jackson, trained in documentaries, enlivens the script with warm human touches.

8
A Man Escaped

A nuclear power station is about to explode, though this quaint production from the Children's Film Foundation treats the matter as a minor domestic hiccup. Cast members include John Forgeham, former *Crossroads* luminary, and the reliable Dudley Sutton.

9
Stranger on the Third Floor

Stark, true story of a French Resistance fighter escaping from a Gestapo prison, much of it shot on the authentic location. Bresson's trademarks are all here: non-professional actors; scenes scrubbed clean of unnecessary detail; uplifting intensity.

Matching Titles: Films

These films have all been shown recently on British television.

Warm-up

What are the advantages of watching films on television compared with going to the cinema? What are the disadvantages? Which do students prefer? In a wider context, is television killing the cinema? What is the state of the native film industry in students' own countries?

Telling a good joke is serious business

LAUGH and the world laughs with you, weep and you weep alone. It isn't always true though. We don't always laugh together. Humour can divide just as much as it can provide a sense of fellowship.

Psychologists are fond of saying that jokes are a form of release – under the guise of cracking a good one, fears are dispelled and hostility becomes socially acceptable.

But is it that simple? Some of the wittiest people and some of the funniest jokes leave one not with the feeling that the world is full of happy laughter and harmony, but pinpoint a very nasty side of life's cruelties and divisions.

There is absolutely no comfort, for example, to be had in Dorothy Parker's cuttingly short remark on Katharine Hepburn's performance in a Broadway play – "She ran the whole gamut of the emotions from A to B."

It tells you less about Miss Hepburn than Miss Parker. Miss Parker has come out on top, which is surely why the wit – who will be out in force again today, as usual, in every office, propping up every bar, out on every factory floor – earns respect and admiration.

Original wits are few and hard to come by. The next best thing is to tell jokes. All you have to do is get the punchline in the right place and you could be top dog, too. Have *you* heard the one about the Irishman who . . . ?

But what's so funny about Irish jokes? Sooner or later, someone was bound to take the thing seriously and write a paper on The Irish Joke As A Social Phenomenon and now it has happened. Christie Davies, Professor of Sociology at Reading University, is to present his work at the annual meeting of the British Association for the Advancement of Science in Belfast.

He says the British are not as cruel as the "molto-fortissimo white liberals", at whom he pokes fun, like to maintain. He has compiled a long list of countries with an equivalent of the Irish joke – all with a similar line in poking fun at the so-called stupidity of a neighbouring country or a local ethnic minority.

Connoisseurs of the Irish joke will, no doubt, particularly appreciate the South African jokes about Van Der Merwe, the Afrikaner. Instead of "The Irish attempt to climb Mount Everest has failed – they ran out of scaffolding", try the one about Van Der Merwe being put in charge of a new integrated bus taking foreign visitors around Pretoria.

He explains: "I know you all think everything is segregated by colour in South Africa, but it isn't true on my bus. As far as I'm concerned you can all be green. Right then, everyone on board, light green at the front, dark green at the back."

As Professor Christie points out, it is no coincidence that the butts of these jokes are never those neighbours with whom the joke-telling nation has ever fought a major war. Nor do his observations show that those who are laughed at for their stupidity are, in truth, particularly stupid or particularly dislikable.

The universal popularity of this kind of joke, he says, can be explained by the fashion in which the teller comes out with a sense of "playful superiority". For the key to each joke is that once the British begin to relate a story about an Irishman, the French about a Belgian, the Americans about a Pole or even the Irish about a man from County Kerry, you know these tales are going to be about stupidity.

The prime feature of all these jokes, he says, is how closely related those who tell them are to their victims. "For the joke-tellers, the butts are either the closest and most familiar of neighbours, the most remote and provincial of their own people or long-established and half-assimilated minorities."

Have you heard the one about . . . ?

There is nearly always a linguistic superiority in these jokes, too. They are not 130 chauvinistic in the sense that one is ever laughing at a foreign language – the butt of the joke speaks the same language but in a comical fashion. The teller is always on the high ground, because his is the dominant language or culture.

There is, apparently, "weak evidence" to show that the Ir- 140 ish joke is not one of total rejection. In many British jokes about the Irish, says Professor Christie, the victims are often wits, rather than half-wits. Mainland skill at poking fun at the generations of immigrants from the bogs, in their traditional role as underdog and always confused in sophisti- 150 cated England, has constantly been cut down to size by the altogether more brilliant Irish gift for laughing at themselves.

Country where jokes about stupidity are told	People about whom the jokes are told
Britain	Irish
United States	Poles (and locally other groups)
Canada (Ontario)	Newfoundlers (Newfies)
Canada (West)	Ukranians
Australia	Irish, Tasmanians
New Zealand (North Island)	Irish, Maoris
New Zealand (South Island)	Irish West Coasters
Ireland	Kerrymen
South Africa	Afrikaners (Van der Merwe)
France	Belgians, Swiss (Ouin-Ouin)
Netherlands	Belgians, Limburghers
Germany	Ostfrieslanders
Sweden	Finns, Norwegians
Italy	Southerners
Switzerland	Fribourgers
Greece	Pontians (Black Sea Greeks)
Austria	Carinthians, Burgenlanders
Russia	Ukranians
Iran	Rashtis (Azerbaijanis from Rasht)
Iraq	Kurds
Israel	Kurdish Jews
Egypt	Nubians
India	Sikhs (Sardarji jokes)
Brazil	Portuguese

Telling a good joke is serious business

A   The Vocabulary of Humour

1   After reading the article right through, see if you can find the word or phrase which best fits the following definitions or situations:

    a   A person who can use words in a clever or amusing way.
    b   The final line of a joke, which makes everyone laugh.
    c   The 'victim' of a joke, the person a joke is told against.
    d   'Make fun of' is similar to '_____ fun at'.
    e   A common way of beginning a joke.

2   The following words, not in the text, are also connected with humour. Do you know what they mean?

    a   slapstick   *f*   a standing joke
    b   a comedy   *g*   a hoax
    c   a farce   *h*   a pun
    d   a practical joke   *i*   a laughing stock
    e   a sick joke   *j*   a shaggy dog story

Discuss with a partner before checking in your English–English dictionary.

B   Pronunciation

Does the word *laugh* rhyme with
a   loaf?   *c*   scarf?
b   bath?   *or d*   south?

C   Talking Point

Is your country mentioned in either of the lists given? If not, which group of people do you tell jokes about? (Or perhaps others tell jokes about you!) Do the facts in your case fit Professor Christie Davies' analysis?

Telling a good joke is serious business

This piece about the psychology of humour is analytical in parts and perhaps more suited to higher-level students.

Warm-up

Ask if anyone knows any jokes in English. Ask if they know what an 'Irish' joke is. Do they tell jokes 'against' any particular group of people or culture?

Supplementary activities

1   Don't forget to have your own joke-telling session – not necessarily about minority groups. Students get a lot of intellectual pleasure from telling (and understanding) even the simplest joke in a foreign language.
2   Use the table as a springboard for a general discussion on the names of countries, the language(s) spoken and the names of the people.

Example

Country	Language Spoken	People	Adjective
Spain	Spanish (also Basque and Catalan)	Spaniards	Spanish
Germany	German	Germans	German

Secretaries: the wasted asset

Bosses who restrict their secretaries to tea and
typing squander greater potential skills.
ALAN ROAD reports.

TOO MANY British mana-gers cannot manage their own secretaries. That is the opinion of Juliet Hepburn, who began as a secretary and is now lead-er of a campaign to maximise the use made of a much under-rated group of employees.

10 The campaign is being run by the Industrial Society – an organisation with 16,000 mem-bers, including trade unions – which aims to increase the pro-ductivity and profitability of British businesses.

It would seem indefensible to squander the time and ta-lents of so many secretaries by confining them to the tradi-

20 tional typing and tea-making activities.

Among the most popular of the 2,000 courses and confer-ences staged each year by the society is one entitled 'Helping Your Manager.' Four years ago, when it began as a two-day course for secretaries and bosses, the project limped

30 along, for the simple reason that bosses were not willing to waste two whole days, as they saw it.

It was when someone – probably a secretary – had the brainwave of continuing the two-day course for secretaries, but bringing in the managers at lunchtime on the second

40 day, that things began moving – so much so that the society now runs a dozen such courses a year in London and through-out the country, and has had to double its advisory staff to cope with the extra work.

Lingering doubts its spon-sors might have harboured over the need for such a course

50 were soon dispelled. Shock-horror tales of bad office prac-tice began to emerge like copies from a duplicator ...

and often they were as repeti-tious.

There were the bosses who banged on adjoining walls to summon secretaries, says Mrs Hepburn, and others who re-

60 fused to divulge details of their day's programme, or even their whereabouts.

A common source of fric-tion was the morning mail. There was one boss who in-sisted that when he was on holiday his letters should be forwarded to him in More-cambe, and another who

70 would not allow his secretary to open his letters even when he was at work. After pressure brought to bear during the course, he agreed that this might be unreasonable, but a follow-up inquiry from the

society revealed that he was allowing his secretary to open the letters, but only in his

80 office and under his beady eye. Progress can sometimes be slow.

A senior secretary in a law firm, who had opened every-one's mail since the days when the total staff was two partners and herself, continued to do so when they had expanded to employ 50 secretaries. The re-

90 sult was that the morning mail never arrived on desks before 3 p.m.

On a more personal level Mrs Hepburn and her col-leagues have been appalled by the number of managers who do not make time to talk to their secretaries on a regular basis. 'Everybody else can

100 have five minutes of the boss's time, but it's never convenient for the secretary.'

Even when some enterprising girl makes her own appointment in the diary, that is always the one that is cancelled because of pressure of work. Small wonder that the turnover of secretaries in some 110 companies is 60 per cent in a year.

'All you need to avoid this waste is to invest a little time in motivating secretaries to realise that they are part of the management structure,' Mrs Hepburn insists.

Secretaries often arrive on the course worried that their 120 shorthand and typing skills will not stand up to scrutiny. They find that the subject is rarely, if ever, mentioned.

Instead, they are questioned first about their perceptions of themselves. 'Too many think of themselves as *only* a secretary – an adjunct to, rather than a part of, the management 130 team,' says Mrs Hepburn.

Next the secretaries are encouraged to use their initiative, to anticipate problems rather than to sit at their desks twiddling their thumbs. There is talk about office administration – making appointments, controlling a diary and evolving a system for keeping track 140 of earlier decisions.

The importance of communicating – through letter-writing, the telephone and face-to-face meetings – is emphasised. 'An awful lot of secretaries would never shake hands with a visitor,' Mrs Hepburn says.

When the bosses join the 150 course during an informal lunch on the second day, their reactions never vary. 'They walk straight up to their own secretaries and ask, with an embarrassed grin: "What have you been saying about me?"'

Secretaries: the wasted asset

A   Comprehension

After reading the article right through, try and answer the following questions.

1   Why was the two-day course 'Helping Your Manager' a failure when it was first put on?

2   What happened to make the course successful?

3   In what ways, according to what was revealed on the courses, do managers sometimes
    a   abuse their secretaries?
    b   under-use their secretaries?

4   How is it suggested that managers should improve the use they make of their secretaries?

5   How can secretaries help themselves?

B   Vocabulary

1   Find words in the text with a meaning similar to each of the following:

    a   not valued highly enough (page 96,   e   to handle (page 96, column 1)
        column 1)   f   to reveal (page 96, column 2)
    b   to waste extravagantly (page 96, column   g   extremely shocked (page 96, column 3)
        1)   h   close examination (page 97, column 2)
    c   restricting (page 96, column 1)
    d   (a) brilliant idea (page 96, column 1)

2   First, check your answers to the previous exercise.
        Then read the article again, this time concentrating on vocabulary not already covered and which is new to you. Discuss the meanings with your teacher or look up the words in your (English–English) dictionary.
        Now try the following exercise, which is really like a test. The sentences are all taken from the article, but some key words have been left blank, with just the initial letters given. Can you fill in the gaps? The approximate meaning of each sentence is written underneath to guide you. No looking back until the end!

    a   *Juliet Hepburn is now leader of a campaign to m_____ the use made of a much u_____ group of employees.*
        Juliet Hepburn is now leader of a campaign to make the most use of a group of employees who are not appreciated enough.

    b   *It would seem i_____ to s_____ the time and talents of so many secretaries by c_____ them to the traditional typing and tea-making activities.*
        There can be no justification in wasting the time and talents of so many secretaries by restricting them to the traditional typing and tea-making activities.

    c   *The project l_____ along.*
        The project made slow progress.

    d   *L_____ doubts its sponsors might have h_____ over the need for such a course were soon d_____ .*
        Any uncertainty still felt by the sponsors over the need for such a course soon disappeared.

e *There were the bosses who b_____ on adjoining walls to s_____ secretaries, and others who refused to d_____ details of their day's programme, or even their w_____ .*
There were the bosses who knocked loudly on adjoining walls to call their secretaries, and others who refused to reveal details of their day's programme, or even where they were going to be.

f *Small w_____ that the t_____ of secretaries in some companies is 60 per cent in a year.*
It's not surprising that in some companies 60 per cent of secretaries leave every year.

g *Secretaries often arrive on the course worried that their shorthand and typing skills will not s_____ u_____ to s_____ .*
Secretaries often arrive on the course worried that their shorthand and typing skills will not bear close examination.

h *Next the secretaries are e_____ to use their i_____, to a_____ problems rather than to sit at their desks t_____ their t_____ .*
Next the secretaries are urged to be resourceful, to foresee problems rather than to sit at their desks doing nothing.

C   Pronunciation

1   Look at the paragraph which begins *It was when someone . . .* (lines 34–46). How many words can you find containing the vowel sound /ʌ/ (as in *bus*)? (Don't include *but*, which is usually pronounced with the schwa sound /ə/.)

2   Look at the paragraph that begins *A common source of friction . . .* (lines 63–82). How many words can you find containing the vowel sound /ɔː/ (as in *sport*)?

3   Look at the paragraph that begins *Next the secretaries are encouraged to use their initiative . . .* (lines 131–40). Copy this paragraph out and mark the stressed syllables by putting a line under the appropriate vowel letter(s).
   E.g. *N**e**xt the s**e**cretaries are enc**ou**raged . . .*

D   Discussion

There are many more female managers now than there used to be.

1   Do you think women know how to 'manage' their secretaries better than men do?

2   Do you think that secretaries on the whole prefer to work for a man or for a woman?

3   How do men react to having a woman for a boss?

Discuss in class, in small groups, or with a friend.

E   Writing Activity

1   Basing your work on your reading of the article, prepare and design a leaflet or poster, for distribution to managers, on how to treat a secretary.

For example: *If you need to call your secretary, don't bang on the wall! Why not install an intercom?*

2 Design a similar leaflet, but this time give your message more point by being ironic.
For example: *Always bang on the wall when you need your secretary – she loves the vibrations!*

In each situation work in pairs or small groups if possible. Try to make your work eye-catching, and use the talents of anyone artistic in your group. Remember to check your English with your teacher before copying out the finished version.

Secretaries: the wasted asset

This article is written in a straightforward, open style, and has plenty of concrete examples to support its theme. However, it does have some challenging vocabulary, and this is highlighted in the exercises.

Warm-up

Ask if anyone has ambitions to become a secretary. If so, why? What do they think the job of a secretary involves/should involve? How well paid are secretaries? How well regarded are they in different countries? (What is their status in society?) Have attitudes of bosses changed or not in recent years?

B   Vocabulary

2   After reading the article again, make the discussion of vocabulary a question and answer session, with the class asking the questions. Be prepared to give other examples of the use of 'new' words. Discuss, if you think it necessary, the meanings of any key words used in questions a–h and not already brought up by the class. Use the answers to the exercise as a checklist. Give the students time to absorb the new words (and their spellings!), perhaps as homework, before giving the test exercise.

C   Pronunciation

1   Students often mispronounce the considerable number of words spelt with 'o' and 'ou' but which have the vowel sound /ʌ/.
2   The diphthong /ɔə/ is nowadays rarely heard, and many modern dictionaries don't list it at all. The six words here would all have the monophthong /ɔː/ in present-day RP.
3   After checking the marking of the stressed syllables, get students to read the paragraph aloud. You could practise chorally first of all, with students then practising in pairs before being asked to perform 'solo'.

Matching Headlines

Here are nine more news stories, but this time all eighteen words of the headlines have become jumbled up. Can you sort them out? You should be able to find a two-word headline for each of the nine news items.

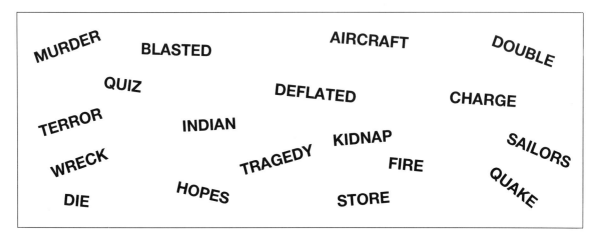

MURDER   BLASTED   AIRCRAFT   DOUBLE

    QUIZ   DEFLATED   CHARGE

TERROR   INDIAN   SAILORS

WRECK   TRAGEDY   KIDNAP   FIRE   QUAKE

DIE   HOPES   STORE

Twenty people were injured evacuating a chartered jet which caught fire landing at Dublin.

1

A huge earthquake, measuring seven on the Richter scale, shook the India–Tibet border early this morning.

4

Police questioned a third man about the alleged kidnap of baker Michael Varone in Peterborough last week.

7

Nineteen crewmen died and only one was rescued when a Maltese-registered cargo ship sank off Barcelona.

2

Surgeons failed to save the unborn baby of a Shropshire woman who died after a car crash near Nantwich, Cheshire.

5

Navy divers blew up part of the sunken World War II cargo ship Breda off Oban, Strathclyde, to stop divers removing dangerous ammunition.

8

Five supermarket workers were killed and two wounded in a robbery in the US city of St Louis.

3

The German entry in the first transatlantic balloon race, weighed down by ice and heavy rain, made an emergency landing in rough seas about 740 miles off Newfoundland. Its two pilots were picked up unharmed by a tanker.

6

Four pop musicians were remanded in custody at Willesden magistrates court, London, charged with the murder of Clement Henry at his Wembley home last Monday.

9

Matching Headlines

See General Note on page xii.

Note: 'Kidnap Charge' and 'Murder Quiz' are not possible, since the police only questioned a man about the kidnapping – they did not arrest him.

Quiz 2

Here is another quiz, based on the second half of the book. See how quickly you can find the answers.

1 Who is Director of Operations for British Airways?

2 How old is Mrs Jennifer Guinness?

3 Who is the editor of the New Scientist?

4 Whose portrait hangs in the Cabinet Room of Number 10 Downing Street?

5 How many staff does 'Cycling for Softies' have in France?

6 What is the name of Chelsea's goalkeeper?

7 Who is the crime correspondent of the *Daily Telegraph*?

8 How long does it take to fly from Australia to Britain by Cathay Pacific?

9 How much does a Red Arrows jet cost?

10 What is the name of the firm of architects responsible for a new design of skyscraper?

11 In what country are jokes about Portuguese people told?

12 Who is the director of ASH?

13 At what address was Mrs Jennifer Guinness held by kidnappers?

14 Who has got ten points from six matches?

15 How big is the area of the Algonquin Provincial Park?

16 Who provided money for the 'Coexistence project'?

17 Whose girlfriend got a job dancing in Beirut?

18 Who gets nervous before an ice-hockey match?

19 How many members has the Industrial Society?

20 Who is the producer of The Natural History Programme?

Suggestions for using the Quiz

See also General Note on page xii.

1   Students complete the quiz individually, writing down their answers. The first with an all-correct solution wins. (Collect papers in order of completion; the answers are very short, and easy to mark on the spot.)

2   As above, but students work in pairs.

3   Divide the class into two or more groups, and read out the questions in turn. Students call out the answers as soon as they find them (or, possibly, remember them!), the first correct answer scoring two points for the team. Deduct a point for any incorrect answer called out (this discourages wild guessing!). Students should have their books open at the Contents page – not the Quiz page!

ANSWER KEYS

Unit 1 – Matching Headlines

[1 RACIAL ACCORD]   **4** SKIERS HURT   **7** DOUBLE TROUBLE
2 FLAT KILLING   **5** FERRIES HIT   **8** HOTEL BLAST
3 GALLERY RAID   **6** FALLOUT LINGERS   **9** MURDER PROBE

Unit 2 – A Heavenly Piece of Kentucky Fried Chicken

A Comprehension

1c, 2b, 3c, 4a, 5b

B Vocabulary

1 **a** *hoardings*
   b *bespectacled*
   c *vast*
   d *a joint venture*

   e *tucking in* (*into* is used if a noun follows, as in the text).
   f *finger-lickin' good* (*lickin'* – instead of *licking* – is used to indicate American pronunciation, and is the standard spelling of the slogan).

2 **a** *scarf*   **b** *cymbal*   **c** *lion*
3 This is a double pun or 'play on words'.
   a *Heavenly* has two references:
     – it means *delicious*, referring to the chicken;
     – it is a reference to the Gate of Heavenly Peace, in Peking (lines 28–9).
   b *Piece* and *Peace* have the same pronunciation.

C Grammar

It doesn't taste bad.

Unit 3 – Zombie on the road

Matching Exercise

Don't eat a heavy meal before driving.
Talk to passengers but not to the point of distraction.
Keep your eyes moving and check your rear-view mirror often.
Take an interest in all road signs and traffic around you.
Don't try to drive too far in one day.
Keep the temperature in the car cool.
Avoid driving during normal sleeping hours.
Take a coffee or walking break every hour or so.
Wear comfortable clothing.

ANSWER KEYS

Vocabulary

1 *mesmerising, hypnosis, trance-like, fatigue, somnolence, (to) nod off*
Note: *Drowsy* and *drowsiness* are not actually used in the article, but are worth introducing in this context.

2 It comes from the expression *to have forty winks* – to have a nap.

Discussion

Danger of mechanical failure or a tyre blow-out at high speed; fog; heavy rain (danger of aquaplaning); high winds; contra-flow systems, especially at night; slow-moving vehicles; multiple pile-ups through unforeseen hazards (fog, earlier accident, lanes being 'coned off' for repair and thus forcing traffic to converge), etc.

Unit 4 – Some people love it – some people don't!

A   Matching Exercise

PICTURE	A	B	C
TEXT	**3**	**1**	**2**
COMMENTS	**b**	**c**	**a**

C   Pronunciation

1 *aerobic, scared, area*
2 *experience, period, seriously, clearly*
3 *dead, healthy, unpleasant, heavy, health*

Unit 5 – 110-year-old tourist

A   Memory Test

1 110
2 Swansea
3 Paddington
4 A red rose
5 A (coal) miner
6 Because he couldn't afford the fare
7 The Houses of Parliament
8 People will think he's getting old!
9 Don't drink, don't smoke and don't curse (swear)
10 76

B   Vocabulary

1 a pleasurable experience, paid for by somebody else!
2 well dressed
3 a tour that makes short stops at a number of places
4 Member of Parliament
5 the separate parts of a mixture
6 to swear or use bad language
7 to begin a journey
8 to make a witty remark or joke

C   Project

Swansea: in Wales, on the south (Bristol Channel) coast;
Aberdeen: in Scotland, on the east (North Sea) coast;
Ilfracombe: in England, on the north Devon coast.

D   General Knowledge

Blackfriars, Cannon Street, Charing Cross, Euston, Fenchurch Street, King's Cross, King's Cross Thameslink, Liverpool Street, London Bridge, Marylebone, Paddington, St Pancras, St Paul's Thameslink, Victoria, Waterloo.

Unit 6 – Jailed umbrella man refused to fold up his brollies and go

A   Comprehension

1   He was the first street trader sent to prison under Westminster City Council's new policy.
2   By having to pay fines.
3   Because the magistrate had seen him before and knew what the answer to his question was going to be.
4   He was able to have a rest and put on some weight.
5   The fact that he missed the opportunity of selling a lot of umbrellas during a very wet period.
6   It means 'I earn enough to live'.
7   Probably because he earns rather a lot and he may not want everyone (including the tax officer!) to know.
8   In the centre – the area around Oxford Street, Regent Street and Piccadilly.

B   Vocabulary

1   a serious promise
2   something bought or sold at a bargain price
3   rapid, fast-moving (here referring to 'trade')
4   shy, holding something back
5   to reveal
6   to free (you get rid of something, but you rid a place or person of something)

Unit 7 – Sayings of the famous

1   Luciano Pavarotti
2   Mikhail Gorbachov
3   Boris Becker
4   Terry Anderson
5   Frank Sinatra
6   Queen Elizabeth II
7   John Major
8   Katharine Hepburn
9   Prince Philip, Duke of Edinburgh
10   Lady Thatcher
11   Bob Dylan
12   Jimmy Connors
13   Pope John Paul II
14   The Duchess of York
15   Ferdinand Porsche
16   General Schwarzkopf
17   Woody Allen
18   The Princess of Wales

Unit 8 – Get to work on a summer job

A   Scanning Exercise

1 Norway   **2** £16   **3** 17   **4** An International Student Identity Card   **5** £8.80   **6** St Albans
7 25   **8** About £80   **9** Holland   **10** Oxford   **11** Nothing   **12** Before

B   Vocabulary and Abbreviations

1   work on an archaeological site
2   accommodation and meals
3   a stamped addressed envelope
4   the Youth Hostels Association

5   an express train
6   British Rail
7   the Young Men's Christian Association

Unit 9 – 'Brain trains' give commuters chance to learn Japanese

A   Memory Test

1 'Brain trains'   **2** Ten years ago   **3** Nothing   **4** Anywhere – they are other passengers
5 Three   **6** The south-east   **7** Stickers   **8** Japanese   **9** Glasgow to Edinburgh   **10** Japanese, palaeography, human biology, American football, antiques, psychology, architectural history, accountancy, law.

Unit 10 – Cartoon

The correct sequence is 3, 5, 4, 2, 7, 1, 6

Unit 11 – The Great Hurricane (1): Battle against the disaster in the night

the country was paralysed
trees were uprooted
windows were smashed
roofs were torn off
garages were demolished
cars were crushed

caravan parks were wrecked
buildings were damaged
the elderly were evacuated
roads were blocked
traffic was diverted

The five other past participles used in the text to describe a state of damage to cars are:

wrecked (headline)
destroyed (lines 15–16)
abandoned (line 23)

broken (line 46)
smashed (line 101)

Unit 12 – The Great Hurricane (2): Nearest to nuclear war

A   General Comprehension

2

B   More Detailed Comprehension

1   A military siege.
2   It resulted in their being completely cut off from the outside world.
3   Because he doesn't stick to all the rules and regulations.

C   Vocabulary

1   **a** *a gang*   **b** *a fortnight*   **c** *a detour*   **d** *a tip*   **e** *a crane*
2   **a** to employ   **b** to communicate in order to co-ordinate work   **c** to pull heavy objects   **d** to see or observe   **e** to increase
3   **a** a large mechanical digger   **b** the Women's Royal Voluntary Service   **c** the people who work at the Meteorological Office, or Weather Centre, i.e. the weather forecasters   **d** a type of pullover or sweater   **e** local taxes

D   Grammar

1   Had there been more experienced foresters available . . .
2   Had the storm happened during the day . . .
3   Had the roads not been blocked . . .
4   Had the men at the council tip not opened the gates . . .

Unit 13 – Matching Titles: TV Programmes

1   Top of the Pops   4   The Dream Machine   7   The Natural World
2   Tomorrow's World   5   The Clothes Show   8   Food and Drink
3   The Sky at Night   6   Making Their Mark   9   Singles

Unit 14 – Why the stars of rock who sing of their pain might actually mean it

A   General Comprehension

1   Emotional pain – for example, of love or loneliness – and the physical pain caused by laryngitis.
2   He used his voice too much when he was young.
3   *Over-use* means 'using too much'; *abuse* means 'using in a harmful way'.
4   Being selective about the work they do, i.e. not undertaking too much; voice training; warming up before a concert; resting the voice afterwards.
5   Forcing the voice; undertaking too much work; smoking; being in a smoky atmosphere; taking aspirin; coughing; taking steroids; an air-conditioned atmosphere; late-night parties after the show!

6 Setting up a special telephone line; making training videos for doctors and running training sessions; setting up specialist centres around the country to give advice.

7 Because if it becomes generally known that they have problems, they will not be engaged by agents.

B Vocabulary

1 The larynx; laryngitis (line 133).
2 In order to be.
3 Gradually return to normal after giving a concert, and rest.
4 A telephone line set up for a special purpose.
5 Injury caused by unnaturally repeated use of a part of the body.
6 *a* a possible danger
     b a performance on stage
     c to ruin
     d arduous, exhausting
     e to give extra energy (here, to make louder)
     f a performance (usually by a pop group or singer)
     g a doctor (General Practitioner)

C Pronunciation

2

Unit 15 – Soothe away care

A Comprehension

1 You wash yourself <u>before</u> you get into the bath.
2 They are too hard.
3 Japan's strangeness is not immediately obvious.
4 Someone who is 'drunk with work' – who loves working and has little time or inclination for anything else.

B Vocabulary

1 *a* hidden *b* walking without picking up the feet *c* obligatory (from French)
     d to be looked after in an extravagant way *e* to lie down
2 *a affluent* *b soothing* *c delectable* *d minute* *e to savour*

Unit 16 – Fishy tale that spans the Atlantic

5, 4, 9, 7, 3, 1, 6, 8, 2

Notes on the correct order

5 – Obvious from the opening words in capitals! Another clue is the use of the present perfect, establishing the significance of the event 'now'.
4 – What does *it* refer to? *A bit of flotsam* in the previous paragraph.
9 – Beginning of the story, after the reader's attention has been arrested by the first two paragraphs. Note the use of the past tenses for the narrative.

7 – The *Star* is a reference to the *Toronto Star* in the previous paragraph.
3 – *The bar* is a reference to the Dunvegan Hotel bar in the previous paragraph.
1 – *He* can only refer to Ralph Cowan in the previous paragraph.
6 – Continues Mr Cowan's explanation.
8 – . . . *$43, which is on its way* clearly has to come before **2** – *Mr McSween . . . is now patiently awaiting his cheque.*

Unit 17 – Memoirs of a secretary . . .

A General Comprehension

1 A system of speed writing using special signs.
2 They couldn't afford to send her to college for very long, so it made her study hard while she was there.
3 Accommodation and food (especially when living with one's parents).

4 Because they are difficult to read back.
5 They took the place of shorthand.
6 A drug.

B Mathematical Questions

1 Thirty shillings (=£1.50).
2 Six shillings (return fare at threepence a day for six days = eighteen pence, which is one shilling and sixpence; five lunches at sixpence a day = 30 pence, which is two shillings and sixpence. Total = four shillings. Subtract from ten = six shillings.)

3 $2\frac{3}{4}$ old pence (approximately one new penny!) (10 shillings, which is 120 pence, divided by 44).
4 One shilling (five new pence).

C Kings and Queens

Victoria, Edward VII, George V, Edward VIII, George VI, Elizabeth II.

D Vocabulary

1 to free from restrictions
2 bold
3 to write down quickly
4 socially obligatory (from French)
5 extremely little

6 to absorb, take in completely
7 to understand a code
8 to waste
9 object of extreme hatred
10 to become popular

Unit 18 – Matching Headlines

1 PLANE DEATHS
2 SOCCER PROTEST
3 BOMBE CACHE

4 SAILOR SAFE
5 JUNIOR ROBBERS
6 SEA RESCUE

7 KNOCKED OUT
8 NICE WORK
9 MISERY ENDS

Unit 19 – On foot to the roof of the world

A   Vocabulary

1 humbling	6 fortuitous	11 handsome
2 insignificant	7 seedy	12 religious
3 majestic	8 crucial	13 adequate
4 demanding	9 memorable	14 evocative
5 remote	10 lingering	15 popular

B   Pronunciation

2-syllable words	3-syllable words	4-syllable words
— • • —	— • • • — •	— • • • • — • •
humbling remote	lingering majestic	memorable fortuitous
seedy	adequate demanding	evocative
crucial	popular religious	
handsome		

The 5-syllable word is *insignificant*

Unit 20 – Chairborne aces of the hard court

A   Comprehension

1   The fact that she wouldn't be able to play tennis with them (or so she thought).
2   The ball is allowed to bounce twice.
3   The striker of the ball.
4   The fact that Simon Hatt was so good at the game.
5   *a*   It gives them more time to make their shots.
   b   If they play nearer the net it is very easy to get lobbed.
6   They don't mind at all – that's the idea of the game.

B   Vocabulary

1   *a 2*   *b 3*   *c 3*   *d 1*   *e 2*   *f 3*
2   *a a brainchild*   *b convalescence*   *c to knock up*   *d coaching*   *e qualms*   *f intuitive*

C   Negative Prefixes

impartial, unmusical, illegible, irreligious, unnecessary, inoffensive, innumerate, immortal, unsophisticated, inhospitable, irresponsible, insincere, unmanageable, illiterate, unnatural

The rule is that the whole of the prefix must be added; where the last letter of the prefix is the same as the first letter of the root word, a double letter will result – for example, *unmusical*, but *unnecessary*.

D   Numbers

1 20   **2** 144   **3** 13

Quiz 1

1	Richard Mayer (unit 2)	11	£6 a year (unit 8)
2	Because live shows are wrecking his voice (unit 14)	12	167 Regent Street, W1 (unit 15)
		13	Alice Thomas Ellis (unit 4)
3	£1030 (unit 19)	14	26,545 feet (unit 19)
4	Jeffrey Archer (unit 4)	15	Sir Robert Reid (unit 9)
5	288,000 (unit 1)	16	£3 (unit 6)
6	£1,000 (unit 20)	17	9 Park End Street, Oxford (unit 8)
7	£25 (unit 8)	18	25 (unit 12)
8	1897 (unit 17)	19	£225,000 (unit 18)
9	Before driving (unit 3)	20	Charlie Brown (unit 10)
10	Canary Wharf (unit 13)		

Unit 21 – Triumph of kidnap Jenny

A Vocabulary and Comprehension

1 **b**
2 **a** See dictionary.
   b He had just said that he wouldn't pay any ransom for her release. **Note:** The word *mock* here is really redundant: *feigning anger* is what is meant.
   c *smirk, beam, chuckle, giggle, burst out laughing*, etc.
   d An approach or attitude which relies on gentleness and reasonableness to achieve results.
   e A *lair* is a wild animal's den or home. To *swoop* is to descend at speed, usually to catch something, and is associated with birds of prey – for example, *the eagle swooped on the defenceless rabbit*. Here, the kidnappers' base is called a *lair* because it is both hidden and dangerous, while the police are said to *swoop* because of the suddenness and swiftness of their action in order to catch their 'prey' – the kidnappers.

Unit 22 – Dry days on the lake

A Memory Test

1 c   2 b   3 c   4 a

B General Comprehension

1 The drinking of alcohol is not allowed.
2 Moving sideways with the current or wind.
3 A British person (slang).
4 Twenty.
5 The bright lights of the tall office and apartment blocks of the centre of Toronto.
6 Walk into a tree.

C Vocabulary

1 **a** to approach someone quietly and unseen in order to surprise them
   b to provoke
   c metal which cannot be used for anything except to be melted down
   d to go in the direction of, go towards
   e to relieve or quench thirst
2 **a** *stealthily*   **b** *affable*   **c** *fooling about*   **d** *provisions*   **e** *dazzling*

D Writing Activity

NO radios
NO musical instruments
NO alcohol
NO glass bottles or tin cans

NO food inside tents at night
Use the litter bins
Beware of bears

In order to preserve the peace and beauty of this place, visitors are respectfully requested not to make unnecessary noise and not to play radios or musical instruments. Please do not bring glass bottles or tin cans into the park, and keep the areas tidy by using the litter bins. Do not provoke bears – they are wild animals. If camping overnight do not leave food inside your tent – the bears may be hungry as well as you! The consumption of alcohol is not permitted.

Unit 23 – Cartoon

The correct sequence is **6, 3, 5, 4, 1, 7, 2**

Unit 24 – Drugs gang held after £51 million cocaine seizure

A Vocabulary

1 described   2 re-exported   3 concealed   4 unloaded   5 tampered with   6 welded
7 collected   8 arrested   9 overlooked   10 reconstructed

B Comprehension

1 **a** padlock had been tampered with   **b** fresh paint   **c** hollow ceiling   **d** internal and external heights of the container were different
2 They **a** removed the tiles   **b** cut away the ceiling   **c** replaced the bags of cocaine with bags of grain   **d** allowed the ship to continue its voyage
3 Customs officers waited at Rotterdam for the gang to collect the container and followed them to a caravan site, where they were caught removing the false ceiling.

C General Question

208 kilos approx.

D Grammar

1 If the container's padlock hadn't been tampered with, it wouldn't have been so easy for the Customs officers to open.

2 If the Customs officers hadn't reconstructed the container so carefully, the gang would have (might have) become suspicious.

3 If the Customs officers at Southampton hadn't been so alert, the drugs smugglers wouldn't have been caught.

Unit 25 – Pat takes good care of them

A Vocabulary

1 **a** of smart appearance, referring to face and hair as well as clothes
  b almost, but not quite
  c honoured and congratulated
  d to promise
  e to claim or imply
  f a tie or strong link

2 **a** *top-notch*
  b *handy*
  c *poverty-stricken*
  d *wary*
  e *self-sacrificing*
  f *rows*

3 Someone who dominates another, especially through physical strength or size. The word is often applied to children – for example, a bigger or older child who threatens or hits a smaller or younger one.

B Structure

Pat Mummy has come to Bangladesh, but she hasn't talked to us for two days!

Unit 26 – A case for smokeless zones

A Comprehension

1 It was over-sensitive.

2 That other people's tobacco smoke is a threat to health.

3 Because they had seen for themselves the effects of tobacco smoke on the air conditioning systems they service.

4 **a** It wouldn't receive the co-operation of everyone.
  b It could be found to be illegal.

5 She is suggesting that employers should take preventive measures now and not wait until damage is proved to have been done (as in the case of workers whose lungs, it was realised too late, had been damaged by exposure to asbestos).

6 A no-smoking rule can be included in the employment contract, which can then be legally enforced at any time.

B Vocabulary

a a fire engine

b other people's tobacco smoke

c a way of achieving one's aim through gradual, diplomatic means

d breaking the terms of employment

e inhaling from a cigarette

f an 'impossible' wish

Unit 27 – Matching Titles: Radio Programmes

1 In Touch

2 Jazz Today

3 The Natural History Programme

4 Songs from the Shows

5 Costing the Earth

6 This Week's Composer

7 A Woman's Touch

8 A Good Read

9 Does He Take Sugar?

Unit 28 – Wheels of fortune

A Comprehension

1 As a result of an enjoyable cycling holiday she and her family had in France.

2 You would probably feel a bit tired and hungry after a day's cycling.

3 That they gained their experience of how best to run the business through first making expensive mistakes.

4 They bought a computer.

5 It has released her from dealing with office routine and given her time to think about the business.

6 Good food, rural surroundings, beautiful scenery, wayside cafes, interesting culture.

B Vocabulary

1
  a someone who quits, who gives up easily
  b with one's bank balance in deficit
  c to reject (someone)
  d natural or intuitive feelings; a personal conviction about being right
  e here, it means someone who doesn't like **too** much strenuous activity – the opposite of a 'macho' type
  f it's surprising
  g to realise
  h a holiday which includes travel and accommodation, organized by an agent

2 **a** *turnover* **b** *contentment* **c** *potential* **d** *commitment* **e** *meticulous*
  f *expertise* **g** *costly* **h** *time-consuming*

Unit 29 – Red Arrows jet crashes into row of houses

A Comprehension

The two badly-damaged houses were not occupied. The pilots parachuted to safety – not too badly injured. One jet landed in a field. Although 200 children were playing only 250 yards from the crash and another school was very close by, no-one on the ground was injured.

B   Grammar Writing Activity

1   Linking words

a   The two pilots, both of whom ejected safely, are now recovering in hospital.

b   The residents, some of whom were treated for shock, were very angry.

c   New members, all of whom are highly-experienced pilots, join the Red Arrows team in winter.

d   The Red Arrows use Hawk aircraft, each of which costs £3.5 million.

2   The passive

a   The residents were said to be angry.

b   One pilot is believed to have a broken leg.

c   The Hawks are said to cost £3.5 million each.

d   The new members who join the Red Arrows team are known to be highly-experienced pilots.

e   The flight leader's Hawk jet is said to have been hit by a second jet.

f   The Red Arrows are thought to have been practising a difficult manoeuvre.

g   The houses are not believed to have been occupied at the time of the crash. (Note the position of the negative!)

h   More than 200 children are said to have been playing nearby.

Unit 30 – Deep in domesticity

A   Vocabulary

1 b   **2 b**   **3 a**   **4 c**   **5 a**   **6 c**   **7 a**   **8 b**   **9 a**   **10 c**

Unit 31 – Garden cities hit the heights

A   Comprehension

1   Because residents and office workers will be in the same building, living together.

2   Because it will be built in sections or 'modules', each one with its own garden.

3   Sheets of glass.

4   To prevent high winds from spoiling the garden.

5   **a**   to provide day-long protection from the sun;

   b   to provide solar energy.

B   Vocabulary

1 *radically*   **2** *currently*   **3** *prediction*   **4** *habitable*   **5** *stays*   **6** *funded*

Unit 32 – Teaching scientists to see with the eyes of a journalist

A Comprehension

1 To present a mathematical theorem in an attractive and appealing way.
2 So that the scientists could get to understand the problems faced by journalists.
3 Ones which have human interest – either in relation to the scientists themselves or to people's everyday experience. The stories should also be topical.
4 It may carry an exaggerated headline or may have been cut.
5 Other more newsworthy stories may have crowded them out.
6 He learnt to understand the problems faced by journalists; he came to appreciate their integrity; he had to accept (reluctantly) that journalists must write a 'story'; he acknowledged the fact that a journalist writing about science can have a greater impact than the scientist himself.

B Vocabulary

1 A *fellow*, here, means a person who has an official position at a university – either as teacher or researcher. The scientists were thus given academic status by the use of this title when they went to study the media – TV, radio and the press – in action.
2 It means that they are often criticised. This is a fairly modern expression – you can also *give someone stick* or *a lot of stick*.
3 It means that some scientists strongly disapprove of this advice (to communicate with the public).
4 It means science *in itself*, or *for its own sake*.
5 It means that newspaper stories on scientific topics are not written to be read and appraised by other scientists.
6 **a** see lines 89–94   **b** see lines 149–51   **c** see lines 163–70

C Grammar

1 You might have to resort to taking a taxi/to walking home.
2 You might have to resort to forcing the lock/breaking in through the window/calling the police.
3 You might have to resort to sleeping in the open/on the beach/in a park.
4 You might have to resort to striking/going on strike/taking industrial action.
5 You might have to resort to raising/increasing taxes.

D Pronunciation

1 **a** — · · opposite, journalist, industry, justified, specified, strenuous
  b · — · provided, familiar, department, distorted, persuasion, encourage, elicit, objective

The odd man out is *entertained*, with stress on the last syllable: · · —

2 **a** · — · · apparently, experience, communicate, anathema, appreciate, interpreting
  b · · — · scientific, mathematics, recommended, academic, correspondent

The odd man out is *demonstrated*, with stress on the first syllable: — · · ·

Unit 33 – Wizard Wilsons lift Blues

A   Comprehension and Deduction

1 Stamford Bridge   **2** Brian Clough   **3** Nottingham Forest   **4** Blue (see headline!)   **5** Segers
6 Because he had been playing without any life or energy   **7** Durie   **8** Two   **9** 3–1 (three one) to
Nottingham Forest   **10** Chelsea won 4–3 (four three)

B   Talking about football and other team sports

1   *a* Who's playing?   *b* Arsenal are playing Spurs (or) Arsenal and Spurs
2   *a*   What's the score? (or) Who's winning?
        b   i) nil nil (or) no score   ii) one one (or) one all   iii) two one to Arsenal (or) Arsenal are
              winning two one (or) Arsenal are two one up
3   Who scored for Arsenal?
4   How long have they been playing? (or) What time did they kick off? (or) What time was the
        kick-off?
5   How much longer to go? (or) How much time to go? (or) How much time left?
6   Who won? (or) What was the score?
7   How did Manchester United get on today?
8   *a* home   *b* away   *c* won   *d* lost   *e* beat   *f* lost to   *g* drew with   *h* draw   *i* all

Unit 34 – Cartoon

The correct sequence is **8, 4, 3, 10, 6, 9, 1, 5, 2, 7**

Unit 35 – Shaping up nicely

A   General Comprehension
b

B   Detailed Comprehension

1 Arrive in Better Shape.   **2** Arrive (after your flight) feeling better, in better condition.   **3** *d*
4 The service you receive during the flight.   **5** *b*   **6** *c*   **7** *pampered*   **8** It gives you free use of
London's transport system, both underground and buses.   **9** *a*   **10** The phrase *shaping up nicely*
means 'doing well', especially with reference to someone who is learning a new skill. For example,
How is John getting on with his golf lessons? Oh, he's shaping up nicely. So, Cathay Pacific is 'doing
well', but the use of the verb *shape* is also an indirect reference to the company's slogan *Arrive in
Better Shape.*   **11** It 'taxis'.

C   Vocabulary

1   *a* showing signs of future success   *b* serious thoughts   *c* to try to win (a person)   *d* to have
        an advantage over, be better than   *e* showy   *f* giving oneself (too much!) pleasure and
        comfort
2   *a* *be airborne*   *b* *tedious*   *c* *lessening*   *d* *buff*   *e* *astonishingly*   *f* *child's play*

Unit 36 – Behind the door of 10 Downing Street

A Comprehension

1 The house at the back is built on a steep slope, and so there is a whole area below the level of the Downing Street entrance.
2 The one at the front (paragraph 4, lines 4–6).
3 There is a security check at the entrance to Downing Street from Whitehall, and there is a policeman on duty outside the house. (The uniformed attendant who opens the door cannot really be considered as security.)
4 So that the prime minister can see all the members of his/her Cabinet when they are sitting round it.
5 Effectively Britain's first prime minister, although he didn't have that title at the time (he rejected it, in fact).
6 Doing it 'officially' would have taken too long.
7 Because, in the early days, very few prime ministers lived there.
8 Portraits of all the previous prime ministers.
9 A young person who is good at his/her job (often business, industry or politics) and who is given early promotion to prepare him or her for a future top position.
10 It is too small!

B Vocabulary

1 *a* moving about in a busy way   *b* a mess, confusion – something difficult to put straight   *c* with a warm, friendly and intimate atmosphere   *d* shaky, not very strong   *e* business-like, ordinary – without any frills   *f* heavily supported
2 *a* unexceptional   *b* deplorable   *c* declined   *d* prohibitive   *e* muddled   *f* stringent

C Research Activities

1 Sir Robert Walpole, Sir Winston Churchill, William Pitt the Younger, Lord Chatham, Edward Heath (now 'Sir'), Lady Wilson (wife of Sir Harold), Lady Dorothy Macmillan (wife of Sir Harold), James Callaghan (now 'Lord'), Mrs Thatcher (now 'Lady'), the Chamberlains (Joseph Chamberlain and his wife).
4 Sir Isaac Newton (1642–1727) – discoverer of gravity.
 Sir Humphrey Davy (1778–1829) – inventor of the safety-lamp.
 Edmund Halley (1656–1742) – discoverer of the famous Comet.
5 Chequers (in Buckinghamshire).

Unit 37 – Matching Titles: Films

1 Night in Rome
2 Vera Cruz
3 The Sea Chase
4 Stranger on the Third Floor
5 The Thing from Another World
6 The Journey
7 White Corridors
8 One Hour to Zero
9 A Man Escaped

Unit 38 – Telling a good joke is serious business

A The Vocabulary of Humour

1 **a** *a wit* (lines 33 and 39) **b** *the punchline* (lines 42–3) **c** the *butt* of a joke (lines 93 and 132) **d** *poke* (lines 67 and 145) **e** *Have you heard the one about the Irishman who/the woman who/the vicar who . . .* etc. (lines 45–6).

2 The following are rough-and-ready definitions only, for easy reference. Encourage students to use a good English–English dictionary to find examples.

    a Humour that depends on physical action – for example, circus clowns.

    b An amusing play (**Note:** not 'any' play).

    c A humorous play which depends on misunderstandings and fast action.

    d A joke that involves another person's misfortune.

    e A joke in bad taste – for example, about death and disaster, which offends people's sensibilities.

    f A ridiculous or foolish situation which has been going on for a long time and is widely known about and (therefore) laughed at.

    g Not a joke! A trick to make someone believe something that isn't true and then act upon it.

    h A humorous use of two meanings of a word at the same time, sometimes called a 'play on words'.

    i Someone who does something stupid and is laughed at by others.

    j A joke involving the telling of a long story, with a deliberately weak punchline.

B Pronunciation

c

Unit 39 – Secretaries: the wasted asset

A Comprehension

1 Because bosses didn't co-operate (they thought it was a waste of their time/they regarded it as inappropriate for them).

2 Bosses were not invited to attend until lunchtime on the second day.

3 **a** They call them by banging on the wall.

    b They don't let them open their mail or tell them where they are going. (Also, they don't let them do anything but type and make tea.)

4 They should make time to discuss things with their secretaries and motivate them by involving them in management decisions.

5 By having a higher opinion of their importance to the company; regarding themselves as part of the management team; using their initiative and not just waiting to be told what to do.

B Vocabulary

1 **a** *underrated* (lines 7–8) **b** *to squander* (line 17) **c** *confining* (line 19) **d** *brainwave* (line 36) **e** *to cope with* (line 46) **f** *to divulge* (line 60) **g** *appalled* (line 95) **h** *scrutiny* (line 121)

2 **a** *maximise . . . underrated* (lines 4–8)

    b *indefensible . . . squander . . . confining* (lines 16–21)

    c *limped* (lines 29–30)

d *lingering ... harboured ... dispelled* (lines 47–50)
e *banged ... summon ... divulge ... whereabouts* (lines 56–62)
f *wonder ... turnover* (lines 108–11)
g *stand up ... scrutiny* (lines 118–21)
h *encouraged ... initiative ... anticipate ... twiddling ... thumbs* (lines 131–5)

C Pronunciation

1 *someone* (both vowels!) *lunchtime much runs dozen London country double*
2 *source morning forwarded Morecambe brought course*
3 Next the secretaries are encouraged to use their initiative, to anticipate problems rather than to sit at their desks twiddling their thumbs. There is talk about office administration – making appointments, controlling a diary and evolving a system for keeping track of earlier decisions.

Unit 40 – Matching Headlines

1 AIRCRAFT FIRE
2 SAILORS DIE
3 STORE TERROR
4 INDIAN QUAKE
5 DOUBLE TRAGEDY
6 HOPES DEFLATED
7 KIDNAP QUIZ
8 WRECK BLASTED
9 MURDER CHARGE

Note: 'Kidnap Charge' and 'Murder Quiz' are not possible, since the police only questioned a man about the kidnapping – they did not arrest him.

Quiz 2

1 Howard Phelps (unit 25)
2 48 (unit 21)
3 Michael Kenward (unit 32)
4 Sir Robert Walpole (unit 36)
5 13 (unit 28)
6 Niedzwiecki (unit 33)
7 Neil Darbyshire (unit 24)
8 23 hours (unit 35)
9 £3.5 million (unit 29)
10 Future Systems (unit 31)
11 Brazil (unit 38)
12 David Simpson (unit 26)
13 51 Waterloo Road, Ballsbridge (Dublin) (unit 21)
14 Coventry (unit 33)
15 1,776 square miles (unit 22)
16 The Graham Foundation of Fine Arts, Chicago (unit 31)
17 Jeffrey Bernard (unit 30)
18 Snoopy (unit 23)
19 16,000 (unit 32)
20 Grant Sonnex (unit 27)

Subjects and themes

The numbers refer to Units

Exercise types and activities

The numbers refer to Units

Comprehension	2, 6, 11*, 12, 14, 15, 17, 20, 21, 22, 24, 26, 28, 29, 31, 32, 33, 35, 36, 39
Dialogues	4, 6, 28, 33
Discussions (See also Talking points)	2, 3*, 26, 30, 32, 39
Gap-fill exercises	19, 24, 32, 33, 39
Grammar (See separate index)	2, 4*, 11, 12, 24, 29, 32, 33
Jumbled paragraphs (See Sequencing exercises)	
Matching exercises	1, 3, 4, 7, 11, 13, 18, 27, 37, 40
Mathematical questions	17, 20, 24
Memory tests	5, 9, 22, 32, 39
Multiple choice exercises	2, 12, 20, 22, 30, 35, 36, 38
Pronunciation	4, 14, 19, 32, 38, 39
Research activities	5, 17, 36
Role-plays	4, 6, 12, 17, 21, 25, 28, 35
Scanning exercises	8, 11*, quizzes
Sequencing exercises	10, 16, 23, 34
Speaking activities**	5, 7, 8, 15, 31, 32
Talking points (See also Discussions)	8, 9, 31, 36, 38
Vocabulary	2, 3*, 5, 6, 8, 11, 12, 14, 15, 17, 19, 20, 21, 22, 24, 25, 26, 28, 30, 31, 32, 35, 36, 38, 39
Writing activities	4, 5, 6, 7, 8, 14, 15, 22, 28, 29, 32, 39

* See Teaching Notes in Self-Study edition
** 'Speaking activities' involve preparing a talk for the group

Grammatical structures

The numbers refer to Units

Grammar exercises

Conditionals	12, 24
Gerund	32
Inversion	12
Passive voice	11, 24, 29
Present simple	4*
Question forms	33
Relative clauses	29

Structures recurring in texts

Passive voice	11, 24
Past simple	11, 21, 22, 33
Present simple	4
Should	14
Used to (implied)	17

Structures practised in language activities

Could (polite request)	35
Future with *I'll*	35
Past simple	8, 12, 21, 33
Present perfect	33*
Present simple	4, 15, 31
Present continuous	6
Question forms	4, 8, 12, 17, 21, 25, 28, 33
Should	26, 30
Used to	17
Will	15